THE HIDDEN TREASURE
OF THE PARABLES

Alfred S. Brown

COVENANT BOOKS

The Covenant Publishing Co., Ltd.,

8 Blades Court, Deodar Road,

London SW15 2NU

First published in 1997

ISBN 0 85205 022 4

The front cover shows the Sower, sowing his precious seed, taken from
The Bible Picture Book by Muriel J. Chalmers and published by Thomas Nelson
and Sons, Ltd.

Printed in the United Kingdom by Staples Printers Rochester Limited,
Neptune Close, Medway City Estate, Frindsbury, Rochester, Kent ME2 4LT

Introduction

Introduction

The Holy Bible is a unique book for it is the only written Word of God. The printed pages of which it is comprised are the work of men but the information they contain comes, not from the minds of men, but from the mind of God. This sets it far above all other books on faith or religion which, in contrast, do originate in the minds of men.

The Bible is thus the only source of truth and knowledge concerning God and His creation. It begins with the record of the creation of all things, animate and inanimate, of life in all its forms. It then records the threat posed to this by the rebellion of mankind who defies God, choosing 'evil and death' rather than 'good and life' which was the option available to him. The reconciliation of man with God thus became necessary and the means for this was, in the foreknowledge of God, heralded in the early pages of the Bible narrative in *Genesis,* ch.3 v.15.

The influence of the anti-God power continues in the affairs of mankind whose actions in opposition to the will of God bring judgement upon him. The flood brings an abrupt end to that first phase of human development but the descent of mankind is continued in the family of Noah. His descendants also succumb to the same evil influence and further judgement is imposed by God, being this time the destruction of their means of communication, which was their common language. The effect of this traumatic experience is difficult to imagine but it would set back the clock of human knowledge and achievement to the extent that mankind would have to relearn the rudiments of life and self-preservation.

That such an experience in human history occurred is evident from archaeological excavations which took place at biblical Jericho. As the excavators dug into the past each layer of the stages of civilisation proved more primitive the deeper

4

they dug until they reached the layer of stone-age man. As they dug further, expecting to unearth even lower forms of human life, they uncovered the remains of a large city with all the signs of a well-developed civilisation having existed there. Such evidence of a dramatic interruption in the development of civilisation in man's history is in harmony with the biblical record and at odds with the evolutionary hypothesis.

To this point the Bible has been comparatively brief and general in its record of the history of mankind. From *Genesis* ch.12 onwards it becomes more detailed and particular. It now records the Divine plan to overcome man's rebellious nature, with a kingdom of people, selected from among the nations, being the main instrument in God's hands for that purpose. The Bible covers nearly four thousand years of that kingdom's history in which it is trained and nurtured for the fulfilment of its destiny. Some of its history is recorded in the years of its occurrence but some is pre-recorded, or told before it happens and is thus prophetic.

The interpretation of these prophetic passages of Scripture has caused many Bible students over the years to produce diverse conclusions regarding their meaning, which often does not stand the test of time or history. The reason for this is the failure to accept that the Bible is a record of God's dealings with a nation of people to whom He made certain unconditional covenants and promises regarding their future existence.

Many details concerning the future of this nation of Israel were given prophetically, both during her occupation of the promised land and later when, as a divided nation, the resultant two kingdoms were subject to foreign dominance. Particular individuals were given the task of prophesying to the people, often a thankless task, and they on occasions illustrated their message with a parable. In the New

Testament Jesus Christ, the Son of God, also used parables to illustrate the prophetic messages He frequently gave. He usually prefaced them with the words: "The kingdom of heaven is like...(etc.)..."

At the time of our Lord's ministry four languages were in use among the people, these being Hebrew, Greek, Latin and Aramaic. Our Lord often spoke in Aramaic for it was the language of the 'common people' whom He most frequently addressed. When the gospel writers recorded what they saw and heard they did so using the Greek language.

In Matthew's gospel the writer always refers to the kingdom as "the kingdom of heaven," in contrast to "the kingdom of God" referred to in the gospels of Mark and Luke. The difference is in the translating, Matthew giving a very literal translation from the Aramaic while the two other writers give what might be called an equivalent translation. Both translations, however, confer Divine authority over the kingdom so, in this respect, they are synonymous terms.

This, then, is the main subject of the Bible from *Genesis* to *The Revelation,* the kingdom of God on earth past, present and future. Without this understanding much of the Bible may remain an enigma to those who read it and its message will be obscured by consequent erroneous conclusions.

These parables of the kingdom were the subject of a book written in 1931 by the late John J. Morey, so it may seem presumptuous to embark on a further study of them. However, although this study will prove to be basically in agreement with his interpretations of the parables, a further sixty years have passed in which events have not transpired in quite the way he then visualised. Political and military power positions have altered considerably in that time. Technology has changed our lifestyle compared with the 1930s, and not always for the better; our Christian faith has fallen victim to the advance of materialism and multifaith propaganda, so

6

moral decay and apostasy abound. The prophesied signs of the end of the age were of troubles never before experienced, a time of conflict and crisis, a time of despair. Such a time is more evident now than it was in 1931.

In the light of this changed situation a reappraisal of the parables is worth the effort of further study and will prove them to be still relevant in this last decade of the 20th century.

Throughout this study the author has used the *Authorised Version* of the Bible, all the references quoted being taken from it. In the course of the research for this study it became clear that some words and expressions in the parables were a repetition of the same ones used in other parts of Scripture. These proved to be contributory to an overall sense of harmony of thought and purpose in the Word of God, such as is not so revealed in modern translations of the Bible. In the parable of the leaven (*Matthew* ch.13 v.33), where the woman mixes leaven with "three measures of fine meal," the *Good News Bible,* for example, refers instead to "forty litres of flour." In *Genesis* ch.18 v.6, where Abraham asks Sarah to "make ready quickly three measures of fine meal, knead it, and make cakes upon the hearth," the *Good News* version reads: "Quick, take a sack of your best flour and bake some bread."

The sense of harmony and affinity between these Scripture texts (referred to later) has been lost and the sense of Divine inspiration is obscured by such mundane language. These senses of harmony and inspiration are a part of the revelation of God's Word so that, as well as feeding the mind of the reader, his or her spirit is uplifted through the spiritual nourishment it also provides. The mundane language of modern translations will not have the same impact and they are thus of limited value to all who seek enlightenment and understanding concerning the Kingdom of God.

Chapter 1

The Divorced Wife

The Parables of the Kingdom are short yet succinct word pictures revealing different aspects of Israel's history, from her birth in *Genesis* to her maturity as God's Kingdom on Earth under the direct rule of Jesus Christ, as declared in *The Revelation*. They form an important part of the revelation of God's plan for the restoration of mankind from their fallen state, through sin and death, to that perfect state of oneness with God as it was in the beginning.

The use of this pictorial language commences in the Old Testament where God gives us, in this unique way, clear, overall pictures of the Kingdom which are complementary to the rest of the prophetic words of the Bible. Each parable can be studied in isolation and its meaning and message understood and appreciated. But it is also advantageous to view them collectively for it will then be found that a particular theme becomes apparent to which each makes its contribution.

As this study is concerned with the history of God's people it would seem right to take the parables in their chronological order. This means turning to the prophet Hosea for the first parable relating to Israel. The analogy to the nation is depicted in real-life experiences of the prophet in his own unhappy domestic situation. In this we learn that his wife, Gomer, becomes unfaithful to him and he divorces her.

It is clear from the parable that God uses this husband and wife relationship to indicate the closeness of His relationship with Israel. The same analogy is referred to in *Isaiah* ch.54 v.5 where, in contrast to the declaration "...she is not my wife, neither am I her husband..." (*Hosea* ch.2 v.2), God declares to Israel in prophetic terms: "For thy Maker is thine husband."

When we read the account given in *Hosea* we see that the parable is part of a rather wonderful love story. The analogy brings us in at that point in Israel's history where she has become a divided nation but it is really part of a story which began at the time of the nation's early growth in Egypt. As God has provided us with this husband and wife relationship as an illustration then it would seem reasonable that the normal prelude to such a relationship could be found to have taken place in those earlier years. Thus we perceive Israel as a slave girl under her Egyptian master rescued by the Lord Who has known her, as it were, since she was a child. Reference to that period is made briefly in ch.2 v.15. He frees her from her enslavement and takes her to the Sinai wilderness where he introduces her to a new way of life, a way which will bring her peace and prosperity and freedom from all kinds of afflictions. He makes known His love for her and she responds by agreeing to become His wife and accept all the responsibilities this entails. The marriage takes place and the wedding vows are made; this contract is the covenant relationship between God and Israel entered into at Mt. Sinai. She is then settled in a new home and these happier days are remembered later by the divorced wife when she regrets her foolishness, as stated briefly in ch.2 v.7.

From the time of the Judges to the end of Solomon's reign Israel's history is that of a wife who casts envious eyes on her neighbours over the fence, copying many of their ways and getting reprimanded by her husband for her waywardness. Then, as we read in Scripture, Solomon's renowned wisdom is overcome by the temptations of his alien wives and their false gods which he stooped to worship. As with the head so with the body; for the people followed his example and thus broke the covenant they had made at Sinai.

It is really at this point in their history where the parable of Hosea begins. For this act of adultery the husband, God, divorces His wife Israel, confirmed in ch.2 v.2. Yet His love for His wife is not diminished. After declaring, in the first thirteen verses of that chapter, the reasons for the divorce and the corrective measures He will apply to her, God goes on, from the 14th verse, to declare His undying love for Israel and foretells of a time when He will become rebetrothed to her and, finally, remarry Israel cleansed of her iniquities. This rebetrothal is foretold in the 19th and 20th verses and in the final verse of that chapter the reunion is seen to be fulfilled.

We learn of God's displeasure towards Israel and the forfeiture of their special relationship in the first chapter of *Hosea*. This is signified in the names of the sons and daughter born to Gomer. First she gives birth to a son to be called Jezreel, which means "may God scatter," prophetic of the fate to befall the nation. Then Gomer gives birth to a daughter who is to be called Lo Ruhamah, which means "unpitied," signifying that God will not show mercy to Israel because of her lawlessness but will let her endure her well deserved punishment. Another son is then born who is to be called Lo Ammi, meaning "not my People," for the relationship between God and Israel was broken by her adultery and breach of the covenant.

A knowledge of the Divine law is important for our understanding of this situation. Under this law adultery was the only reason for which divorce was permitted in Israel. After being divorced for adultery a woman could not remarry during the lifetime of her former husband, the marriage vow being a lifetime commitment. Israel was now in this position and thus not free to remarry until her first husband had died. Only the death of our Lord at Calvary released her from this bond and made possible the promised rebetrothal spoken of through Hosea and some of the other prophets. (*Romans* ch.7 vs.1-3).

The significance of Jesus Christ's death and resurrection with regard to Israel can only be appreciated through the knowledge and acceptance of the national message of redemption contained in the Scriptures. This message does not conflict with the gospel of personal salvation through faith in Jesus Christ as the Son of God and our Saviour. Rather it complements that gospel and gives meaning and relevance to parts of Scripture which otherwise have no real point.

But Israel did not know of her husband's death and her release from the bond of the old covenant, her first marriage contract. She had to be found and told about it, for God had cast her out of the family home and left her to wander among the nations. In the 14th verse of ch.2 we read that this will take place:

"Therefore I will allure her and bring her into the wilderness and speak comfortably unto her."

This theme is reiterated in the opening words of *Isaiah,* ch.40:

"Comfort ye, comfort ye my people, saith your God. Speak ye comfortably to Jerusalem..."

The greatest words of comfort for Israel would be the news that she had been redeemed by the blood of Christ shed for her on Calvary, and that she was free to become betrothed to her first husband. This news had to be taken to her and the apostles were given that mission by our Lord when He directed them: "Go not into the way of the Gentiles and into any city of the Samaritans enter ye not. But go rather to the lost sheep of the house of Israel." (*Matthew* ch.10 vs.5-6)

This message of national redemption did not apply to any other nation for only Israel were in covenant relationship with God. For individual people of all nations God gives this promise: "Them who honour Me I will honour..." (I *Samuel* ch.2 v.30)

11

The parable in *Hosea* goes on to the concluding words of that chapter at verse 23:

"...and I will say to them which were not my people, Thou art my people; and they shall say, Thou art my God."

This point in Israel's history has not yet been reached and is still in the future. It is in harmony with the end of the age scene given in *The Revelation* which culminates in the great marriage ceremony, when the bride, Israel, is married again to her first husband who died and rose from the grave to make this reunion possible.

In the third chapter Hosea remarries, Gomer, it is believed, having died. Like her this second wife is also an "adulteress" or more correctly translated, an idolatress, for she also came from the northern, breakaway kingdom and thus typified the state of that kingdom in those days. Hosea pays fifteen pieces of silver for her which, according to the *Companion Bible* notes, was the redemption price for a slave. This surely is symbolic of the price of the redemption which God would pay for His wife Israel, who was like a slave during her period of captivity under the Assyrians and her subsequent migrations before settling in the British Isles, the 'appointed place' referred to in II *Samuel* ch.7 v.10.

There is then a period of engagement during which Hosea orders his newly betrothed not to be unfaithful to him and promises that he will be faithful to her. In this we have the counterpart to Israel in the Isles receiving, via the apostles, the news of her redemption through the death of Jesus Christ and her betrothal to the resurrected Lord. The next verse (4) shows that this time of engagement is symbolic of Israel's period of development before becoming a united kingdom, being for a time without a king or central government or national Christian faith. Finally, in verse 5, we are given the prophecy of Israel's return to the Lord their God and to David their King, Who, in this prophetic sense, is Jesus Christ, taking place "...in the latter day."

In this parable we are given, in a sense, the setting of the scene for the rest of Scripture. Prominent in the analogy is the theme of reconciliation for the kingdom which, for a period of time, had forfeited its place in its relationship with God. This promised reconciliation was only possible through the death and resurrection of our Lord. Thus He is central to the fulfilment of the plan so clearly illustrated in the parable. As we study the other parables in the Old Testament the different illustrations each have the same theme as their central message. Thus they, too, have the same dependence on the atoning blood of our Lord and Saviour for their fulfilment.

Chapter 2

The Potter's Vessel

The next parable to be considered is contained in the book of the prophet Jeremiah. In the first six verses of chapter 18 we read the parable of the potter's vessel. A short and simple analogy whose message, basically, is the promise of the continuity of the kingdom; that its state of ruin is not a permanent one. Jeremiah's prophecy was given when the northern kingdom, the House of Israel, had gone into captivity in Assyria.

If the parable is considered in the light of our knowledge of the pottery-making process it will be seen what an apt medium God chose to convey His message to us; that it fits in so remarkably well with each stage of Israel's history. First there is the selection of the most suitable type of clay to form the vessel required by the potter. For God, in His foreknowledge, Abraham was the most suitable clay. The clay has then to be mixed with water until it becomes the right consistency so that it can then be formed into a vessel. The first part of the process is analogous of Israel's journey from Egypt, her years in the Sinai wilderness and subsequent maturity as a nation in the promised land.

That stage of Israel's development, terminating at the end of Solomon's reign when the nation became divided, covers a period of about one thousand years from the call of Abraham. This observation provides us with a time-scale by which it is possible to recognise significant dates in Israel's progress as each stage in the pottery manufacture is completed.

Solomon's son, Rehoboam, set out to try and reunite the kingdom but through the prophet Shemiah God forbade him to do so, for, as God declared: "this thing is from Me." This milestone in the history of Israel is recorded in I *Kings* ch.12 vs.19-24 and in II *Chronicles* ch.11 vs.1-4. It is the place in the parable where Israel, the vessel, is marred in the potter's hands; marred because God saw that she was not yet suitable for His purpose. In the marring the piece of clay returns to a shapeless mass which symbolises the disintegration of the kingdom and the captivities which eventually followed.

That the same piece of clay was reused for the reshaping of a new vessel clearly signified that Israel had not been cast aside in favour of some other nation or people:

"O house of Israel, cannot I do with you as this potter? saith the Lord..." (*Jeremiah* ch.18 v.6).

In the time-scale the marring and reshaping process would take a considerable number of years. During that period our nation's history records the arrival of the Celts, Angles, Saxons and, finally, the Normans who came in 1066. Known by these new names the scattered tribes had come and settled in the British Isles.

The new vessel is now formed. It then has to be set aside to dry out and harden. It is like a process of consolidation and is suitably analagous of that period in our island's history where the people gradually overcome their differences and antagonisms and, in 1603, become the united kingdom of Great Britain. The final stage in the process is the baking of the vessel in the kiln. This is cool when the vessel is placed inside but then the temperature is raised gradually to a high degree. After a suitable time the vessel will be ready and is removed from the kiln by the potter.

This climax in the pottery manufacture seems appropriate to this end of the age period. As we view with increasing concern the upsurge in lawlessness, political instability and moral degeneracy, along with the threat to all life that man's accelerating technical inventiveness now poses, the expression 'things certainly seem to be hotting up' must be more frequently in out thoughts. We find a similarity to this end-time situation in the prophecy of *Malachi,* ch.4. There he describes world conditions which we can expect to see in these words:

"For, behold, the day cometh that shall burn as an oven."

An example, surely, of the great harmony of thought and expression to be found in Scripture.

Although the parable only covers part of the whole pottery process, by implication it can be followed through to its legitimate conclusion as has been done in this study. Its relevance to Israel's history is thus seen to be entirely fitting. This relevance is apparent in another sense also. God might have used other trades such as carpentry, metal working or weaving, for example, these trades being in operation in those days. But when they are considered it will be realised that each requires various tools to produce the end product. In pottery the craftsman's hands are his only tools.

So here we see how apt the analogy is for Israel is very much in the hands of the potter, the everliving God.

"Behold, as the clay is in the potter's hand, so are ye in mine hand, O house of Israel." (*Jeremiah* ch.18 v.6).

We are in His hands for blessing or for judgement, whichever we most deserve.

Our dependence on God is absolute and perhaps this is borne out, also, in the parable, again only to be seen in the pottery process.

Israel is the clay God chose for His Divine purpose. But you can not make anything with dry clay alone. It has to be mixed with water before it can be shaped into a vessel that can be of some use.

Water is used many times in Scripture with symbolic meaning and it is, perhaps, appropriate to think of our Lord's meeting at the well with the woman of Samaria. He tells her of the living water, the water of eternal life which He alone can provide. It would surely be in keeping with the spirit of the parable to think of such water being used in the forming of the kingdom of God on earth. It is in harmony with the theme of continuity and reconciliation in God's plans for His people Israel and emphasises His overruling power in their destiny.

Chapter 3

The Broken Bottle

It is said that there are exceptions to every rule. So it will be seen in the next parable in this study that reconciliation is excluded, as the Scripture clearly shows.

In *Jeremiah* ch.19 there is the account of the earthen bottle which has to be taken to the people of the southern kingdom of Judah and broken in pieces in their presence. This was a warning of judgement to come to the people because of the great evil in their life-style, which included human sacrifice to Baal. The judgement was to be the destruction of the kingdom, symbolised in the breaking of the bottle:

"Even so will I break this people and this city, as one breaketh a potter's vessel, that cannot be made whole again" (v.11).

Through the prophet God makes clear that the house of Judah had the opportunity of seeing the consequences suffered by the house of Israel for their unfaithfulness but had ignored this lesson. He refers to Judah's treachery in making a pretence at contrition but still persisting in her evil ways, (ch.3 vs.6-12). History records that Jerusalem was eventually destroyed in 587 B.C. and the remaining people of Judah taken as captives to Babylon.

The judgement did not apply to the throne, the royal line descended from king David, for the promise God made to him that the throne and his royal line would continue for all time, (II *Samuel* ch.7 vs.13 & 16) was not annulled.

In the books of Ezra and Nehemiah it is recorded that about forty-three thousand of the house of Judah returned to Jerusalem from their exile to rebuild the temple and parts of the city. Their descendants were the Jews of our Lord's time.

The genealogies of Matthew's and Luke's gospels record the fact that both Joseph and Mary were descendants of king David. Confirmation of the promised continuity of his throne is given in the angel's declaration to Mary:

"And, behold, thou shalt...bring forth a son and shalt call his name Jesus...and the Lord shall give unto him the throne of his father David."

Mary's genealogy goes back to David via his son Nathan. Her husband Joseph's line also goes back to David but via his son Solomon. In that line there was a king called Jechonias of whom it was declared through the prophet Jeremiah:

"...for no man of his seed shall prosper, sitting on the throne of David and ruling any more in Judah."

So Joseph was of that seed barred from ever occupying the throne. Those who deny the Virgin birth of our Lord thus pose the obvious question, did God lie to Mary? Also they must bring into question the sinlessness of our Lord; but it is not in the scope of this study to pursue the ramifications of such unsound speculations.

The Jews of our Lord's time were a remnant of the old kingdom or house of Judah. Many others would have migrated from Babylon and joined their kin from the northern kingdom in their westward trek across Europe. The epistle of James is addressed to "...the twelve tribes which are scattered abroad," indicating that this fact was known to him.

However, as the gospels relate, Jesus found much to condemn in the doctrine and practices of the Jews and their rejection of Him as the Messiah sealed their fate. He thus foretold the final outcome which would befall their inheritance when he declared:

"The kingdom of God shall be taken from you and given to a nation bringing forth the fruits thereof" (*Matthew* ch.21 v.43).

The 'fruits' of the kingdom are the preaching of the Word of God, the gospels of salvation and redemption and the proclamation that Jesus Christ was the promised Messiah; that His supreme sacrifice, previously heralded in the Old Testament ordinances, wipes out the sins of all who profess Him their Saviour and Lord; that He will return again to earth to rule over His redeemed kingdom and bring righteous leadership to a world in turmoil.

The Jews proclaim none of these things. When He came as the Messiah they were looking for a king. Soon He will return as the King of His kingdom, yet the Jews are looking for the Messiah.

History records the destruction of that remnant of Judah in A.D.70 when Titus destroyed Jerusalem and massacred the Jews, bringing to its fulfilment our Lord's prediction. Never again would the descendants of the house of Judah form a separate kingdom in the promised land.

The Israeli State presently occupying that part of the world is not a nation *per se,* it is a state. Very few of its inhabitants are descendants of the original house of Judah but are a racially mixed group of people unified only by their faith or political outlook. Much needless error and confusion has been caused throughout the Christian world by the advent of this new Jewish state in Palestine; needless because the promises of God concerning the everlasting nature of the kingdom and the throne, made to the patriarchs and to King David, are not fulfilled in this recent addition to the nation states of the world.

Chapter 4

The Cedar Tree

In the foregoing our Lord's ancestry on His mother's side establishes His legal right to the throne of David, to which He will one day come. However, the location of that throne and its occupant is the subject of the next parable, in *Ezekiel* ch.17.

The prophet is given a prediction concerning Zedekiah, the reigning monarch of the kingdom of Judah when it fell to the invasion of the Babylonians. In this chapter God points to Zedekiah's rebelliousness in despising the covenant and declares that He will withhold His protection from the king and not prevent him being taken captive with his people into Babylon. Subsequently the king's two sons are murdered and then he is blinded by his captors. Perhaps unknown to the Babylonians the law in Israel stated that if there was no male heir to an inheritance it would pass to the female. Zedekiah had daughters and the elder of these would, therefore, be the rightful heir to the throne in the absence of her brothers. These women were in Egypt with Jeremiah when the captivity of the house of Judah began (Egypt was often a place of refuge for Israelites in times of trouble), and it is to the eldest that the parable relates, given in verse 22:

"Thus saith the Lord God; I will also take of the highest branch of the high cedar, and will set it; I will crop off from the top of his young twigs a tender one, and will plant it upon an high mountain and eminent; In the mountain of the height of Israel will I plant it..."

The highest branch of the high cedar is symbolic of the king, Zedekiah. His young twigs, that part of the tree from which its onward growth would proceed, represents his sons and daughters through whom the royal line could continue. The 'tender one' refers to the daughter who, in the providence of God, would provide the continuity of the Davidic line.

Orthodox teaching declares that the 'tender one' of this analogy refers, prophetically, to the first advent of Jesus Christ. However, from the evidence of the genealogy of our Lord given in Luke's gospel, as already mentioned, He was descended from Nathan whereas Zedekiah was descended from Solomon. Therefore such teaching is seen to be in error from the point of view of lineage. From Zedekiah to Christ's first advent is a period of nearly six hundred years. Again such a lapse in time during which there was no apparent occupant for the throne is not consistent with the promise, given in *Jeremiah* ch.33 v.17, that David would never lack an heir to the throne of Israel. Neither does it fulfil the promise made in the blessing given by Jacob when he said:

"The sceptre shall not depart from Judah, nor a lawgiver from between his feet, until Shiloh come." (*Genesis* ch.49 v.10)

Shiloh is a title and it means Prince of Peace. It obviously refers to our Lord and, as will be seen in the prophecy of *Isaiah* ch.9 v.6, The Prince of Peace is one of the titles held by Him when He comes again. It clearly does not refer to His first advent, for that was not His mission at that time.

The biblical record of Zedekiah's daughters ends when they are in Egypt with Jeremiah. In that same period of time Irish secular history records the arrival in the island of Ireland of an eastern princess with a prophet, a scribe and a large stone. She meets and marries the Heremon, or chief ruler, who is called Eochaidh. His ancestry goes back to Calcol (listed in I *Chronicles* ch.2 v.6), a descendant of Zarah, who was one of the twin sons of Judah. Pharez, the other twin, was the ancestor of king David and, hence of Zedekiah's daughter. So the promise made in *Genesis* ch.49 regarding that symbol

22

of monarchy and authority, the sceptre, is seen to have its historical fulfilment in this union between two descendants of Judah.

According to Irish chronicles the princess was called Tamar. This name had royal associations in Israel's earlier history as it was the name of king David's daughter and of the daughter of Absalom, David's third son. The mother of Pharez and Zarah was called Tamar. (*Genesis* ch.38 vs.11-26)

The succession of Irish kings stemming from that union can be traced to the time in the 5th century A.D. when Fergus II came to Scotland and was crowned king of the Scots at Dunstaffnage in Argyll. He brought with him for the enthronement ceremony the stone which had been used for that purpose by his predecessors in Ireland. It was later moved to Scone in Perthshire by Kenneth II, in A.D.846, and to this day it is called the Stone of Scone. Edward I of England confiscated the stone in 1296 and took it to Westminster and in 1300 the wooden Coronation chair was made, having a compartment built specially to house the stone. There it remained until 1996, when it was returned to Scotland.

In *Genesis* ch.28 there is recorded the dream which Jacob had while resting his head on a stone and in verses 18 and 22 the stone is regarded as a symbol of the promise God had made to him. *"This stone, which I have set for a pillar, shall be God's house."*

Having thus attached such importance to the stone Jacob is hardly likely to abandon it but rather to retain it for the significance it held for him. While there is no specific reference to Jacob's stone in Scripture thereafter, there are references to a stone being of significance in Israel's history.

In *Joshua* ch.24 vs.26-27 a stone is set up as a silent witness to the promises made by the people:

"...for it hath heard all the words of the Lord which He

23

spake unto us; it shall be therefore a witness unto you, lest ye deny your Lord."

In the second chapter of Daniel the prophet gives to Nebuchadnezzar the interpretation of the King's dream. In this the kingdom which was to "stand for ever" was symbolised in the stone which would break in pieces the great image. History records the demise of the Babylonian and succeeding empires, as was foretold in the dream allegory. The kingdom of Israel, re-established in the British Isles, has stood against the aggression of various European powers over the centuries, thus bearing testimony to the faithfulness of God. A significant observation was made by Karl Marx when he said:

"England seems to be the rock against which all revolutionary waves are broken."

The physical evidence on the Stone of Scone points to it being a much travelled piece of sandstone. Yet we know that its movements from place to place have been few in number during the last 2,500 years. The wear seen on the metal rings set into it suggest frequent journeys from site to site, which would be consistent with Israel's movements across Sinai until their settlement in the promised land.

To view the stone at Edinburgh, in its new prominent setting and remember the words of Joshua should be a thought-provoking experience, for it is, indeed, a witness unto us. While the stone itself is a witness so, too, is the occupant of the Royal seat; a continuing witness to the fact of Israel's rejection of God to rule over them in preference to one from among their own people. But Israel is the kingdom of God and the throne is the seat of supreme authority over the kingdom. Thus it is the throne of the Lord and its occupant is merely the regent "until Shiloh comes."

As God has preserved His kingdom on earth according to His great mercy and promise so, too, has He preserved that seat of His authority within the kingdom. His reason for such undeserved favour can be found in the declaration made through the prophet *Isaiah* (ch.43 v.12):

"...therefore ye are my witnesses, saith the Lord, that I am God."

The kingdom is, by its continuing existence, a living witness that the Lord is a covenant-keeping God: "and the heathen shall know that I the Lord do sanctify Israel, when my sanctuary shall be in the midst of them for evermore" (v.28).

In the 23rd verse of Ezekiel's analogy it is declared that the tree, after being planted, would bring forth boughs and bear fruit and "be a goodly cedar." Boughs, of course, are branches coming from the main stem and a study of the British Royal family tree reveals its ancestral links with the royal houses of Europe. This is consistent with the belief that some of the migrating tribes settled in much of the coastland of western Europe where their descendants have remained to this day.

That same verse goes on: "...and under it shall dwell all fowl of every wing; in the shadow of the branches thereof shall they dwell."

British people have, over the centuries, migrated and settled in new lands throughout the world. Any indigenous peoples there have, on the whole, benefited from our influence and mainly Christian lifestyle we introduced. Though British colonial rule was not without its faults those former colonies who have recently opted for self-determination have, in many cases, come under the rule of dictators with the corruption, oppression and loss of freedom this usually entails.

Already quoted has been that verse which refers to "an high mountain ...the mountain of the height of Israel..."

A mountain in biblical terminology is usually a symbol of a kingdom and in the context of the passage it refers to the highest place in the nation in the sense of its spiritual and political status. The capital city of the nation fulfils this as it contains both the throne and the seat of national government. Indeed in the monarch is vested the leadership of both church and state, even if this is now just a nominal rather than an active position. Although the Israel peoples in the British Commonwealth have their own elected governments their ties with the throne are like spiritual cords binding them to the highest point in Israel. It is regrettable, and must be through ignorance and Satanic influence that there is a move towards republicanism in these lands of our Israel brethren. It can, of course, be said that the misguided self-interest of the British government over Europe has, in recent years, given them no encouragement to do otherwise. However, in these last days of this age it should be our prayer that God will remember His covenants and confound the powers of evil which seek Israel's destruction.

This parable portrays the end of the royal dynasty in Jerusalem brought about by the rebellion of Zedekiah. It is perhaps not without significance that the king of Babylon is referred to, earlier in the chapter, as an eagle. In the ensuing ages up to the present time the eagle has figured prominently in European national heraldry. It was used by the Romans and, later, by Austria, Germany and Russia. This emblem has thus been associated with the enemies of Israel throughout much of her history.

The kingdom of God has been the object of Satanic attack from its birth. Its preservation from this continual threat has been accomplished only through the grace and power of God. The parable of the cedar tree is a further example of God's participation on behalf of His people against the powers of evil.

Author's Note:

In Matthew's genealogy Jechonias is the same king who is called Coniah in the Old Testament and the gospel writer declares his period in the history of the kingdom to be: "...about the time they were carried away to Babylon."

It appears to have been the practice of the Babylonian rulers to assert their authority over their captors by changing the names of their kings. Thus it will be found that Coniah's original name was Jechoiachin. After a time as king of Judah he was deposed and replaced by Zedekiah (*Jeremiah* ch.37 v.1). He, too, bore the name given by his captors for his original name was Mattaniah.

Jehoiachin was the son of Jehoiakim who in turn was the brother of Mattaniah. From this relationship it will be seen that the bar to the throne of David placed on Coniah's descendants did not affect the promised continuity of the royal line from Solomon, as it was quite legitmately continued through Coniah's uncle, Zedekiah and, subsequently, his daughter as has been shown.

Chapter 5

The Valley of Dry Bones

The continuity of the royal line being established in Zedekiah's daughter and removed from the threat of extinction in Jerusalem to the safety of the "appointed place" leads us on to the next parable, in *Ezekiel* ch.37. The prophet lived in momentous times, seeing a once proud and prosperous nation disintegrated, cast out of her own land and become captives in the midst of her victorious enemies.

God shows the prophet, in a vision, a valley full of dried up human bones which he is told symbolises the state of the people of Israel. They have ceased to be an ordered community, they no longer have a land of their own, they have lost their identity as a nation and have been reduced to the mere bare bones of a kingdom. In verse 3 of the prophet is asked:

"Son of man, can these bones live?"

He is rather non-committal in his reply: "Oh Lord God, thou knowest."

Ezekiel is then told to prophesy: "Thus saith the Lord..." and in verses 4-6 he prophesies that sinews would be placed on the bones, then they would be covered by flesh and skin and breath put into the bodies. In the vision he sees this take place and the breath of life is breathed into them and they stand up on their feet, "an exceeding great army."

There can be no doubt as to which people are represented in this analogy. In verse 11 the prophet is told: "...these bones are the whole house of Israel" a people without hope and parted from the Lord as a consequence of their unrighteousness.

However, God addresses them through the prophet and declares:

"Behold, O my people, I will open your graves and cause you to come up out of your graves and bring you into the land of Israel."

Thus, in this verse (12) we read of the promise of restoration of the kingdom and of it being taken into "the land of Israel."

In this analogy there would appear to be two stages in this restoration process. The first, and longest in time, is the actual physical restoration of the people which was accomplished in the regathering of the people in the British Isles and the later expansion into the Anglo-Saxon Commonwealth countries overseas. The bones are thus clothed with sinews, flesh and skin and have stood on their feet and become "an exceeding great army."

The second stage is that mentioned in verse 14: "And shall put my spirit in you, and ye shall live, and I shall place you in your own land; then shall ye know that I the Lord have spoken it, and performed it, saith the Lord."

God has not yet put His spirit in us for we are in a rebellious and unrepentant state. Though the Reformation brought a spiritual revival and made the Bible an open book available to everyone the full potential of this God-given gift has not been realised. The proclamation of the earthly kingdom of God has not been given from our churches. Thus error and confusion regarding the form and location of this kingdom have detracted from the relevance of the Word of God to world events and Israel's place within them. But God is not the author of confusion so, when He puts His spirit in us, all false beliefs and teaching will be dispelled and we "shall live" in truth and righteousness as He intended. Then Israel will know that what God foretold through the prophets He will have accomplished through their redemption at Calvary and their restoration to that position where they are once again "My people."

When the Lord Jesus Christ returns in power and glory He will take up His rightful position as King of Israel, fulfilling the prophecy given in *Isaiah* ch.9 v.7. This restoration of the kingdom symbolised in this parable is complementary to the restoration process detailed in the previous chapter of Ezekiel's prophecy. In that chapter the contrast between Israel's degenerate condition, due to her rejection of God, and her restoration to a cleansed and repentant nation is clearly seen. The outstanding point to note in this chapter is the recurrent "I will..." of God:

"I will take away the stony heart out of your flesh, and I will give you an heart of flesh" (v.26);

"And I will put my spirit within you and cause you to walk in my statutes..." (v.27);

"I will also save you from all your uncleannesses..." (v.29).

The picture of the kingdom restored from its former unrighteous and afflicted state to one of peace and plenty is a vision of hope for the future. There is no place for pride or sense of achievement in the kingdom, however, only shame.

"I do not this for your sakes, O house of Israel, but for mine holy name's sake, which ye have profaned among the heathen, whither ye went" (v.22).

Nor is there any doubt how this restored condition will be achieved. "I will yet for this be enquired of by the house of Israel to do it for them" (v.37).

Clearly, then, the restoration of the kingdom will be of the Lord's doing. The vision of the dry bones, explained to the prophet, ends with that assertion:

"...then shall ye know that I the Lord have spoken it, and performed it, saith the Lord."

The prophecy already quoted from Isaiah ends in like manner:

"... The zeal of the Lord of hosts will perform this."

The need for the active participation of God in the process must surely now be evident to all thinking people when we look at the parlous state of the kingdom and of mankind generally. We are in a critical situation, facing potential disaster to all life on earth due to man's lack of wisdom, his greed and lust for power regardless of the consequences. These consequences have become a serious threat to our very existence, to the extent that no human power can save us from them. Only the Divine power of a merciful and covenant-keeping God will save the kingdom and His threatened creation. Our greatest need is for national repentance and the fervent prayer: "come quickly, Lord Jesus."

Chapter 6

The Two Sticks

In the parable of the broken bottle the demise of the house of Judah as a separate kingdom was foretold. However, the two tribes of Benjamin and Judah which formed that kingdom were, and remained, part of the house of Jacob, the collective name for the twelve-tribed nation.

In the providence of God one would expect the house of Judah to be included in the restoration of the whole kingdom of Israel. That this is so is seen in a further parable in that 37th chapter of *Ezekiel*. In the 16th verse the prophet is instructed to take two sticks and write on them the names of the separate kingdoms. On one he had to write:

"For Judah, and for the children of Israel his companions..."

The reference there to his companions signifies those people of other tribes who had remained loyal to the throne and thus become part of the kingdom of Judah. On the other stick he had to write:

"For Joseph, the stick of Ephraim, and for all the house of Israel his companions." Reuben was the eldest of the twelve sons of Jacob but because he did evil in God's eyes he forfeited his position as head of the family, his place being taken by Joseph. Joseph's son Ephraim was then given the position of chief of the ten-tribed house of Israel.

In verse 19 God declares that He will take the two named sticks and join them together so that they "shall be one in mine hand." That which is symbolic is translated to the literal as is seen in verse 21, where we read:

"Behold, I will take the children of Israel from among the heathen (nations), whither they have gone, and will gather them on every side and bring them into their own land."

If one takes God at His word it would be erroneous to spiritualise this passage of Scripture. It so clearly deals with actual people, the people of Israel who have gone into captivity and who, it is inferred, will be dispersed among the nations, thereafter being regrouped in a land of their own. The term "children of Israel" in this verse refers to the dispersed people of all twelve tribes. The return of the comparatively small number of individuals from the Judah captivity, under Ezra and Nehemiah, does not, therefore, fulfil that particular prophecy.

The joining of the two sticks only takes place after the people are gathered together in their own land and have become one nation. Verse 22 declares further that they shall once again come under the rule of one king and that they shall never again be two nations nor two kingdoms. This prophecy of resettlement in a land of their own is further confirmation of the earlier promise made to king David, when there was no thought of moving to another land. Through Nathan the prophet God said:

"Moreover, I will appoint a place for my people Israel, and will plant them, that they may dwell in a place of their own and move no more; neither shall the children of wickedness afflict them any more as beforetime." (II *Samuel* ch.7 v.10)

In appointing this other land which Israel would, one day, occupy it would be in accordance with God's own law that the post-captivity people would not be mixing with an alien race, but, instead, would be settling among their own kith and kin who had arrived at an earlier date. Secular history shows that this was the case, for the language, customs and skills of the people in the British Isles was like those of the scattered tribes who arrived centuries later.

In verse 23 we read about a cleansing process taking place, culminating in the words of God: "...so shall they be my people, and I will be their God." This statement is similar to that given in the prophecy of *Hosea* ch.2 v.23 and is indicative of the time when Israel will have returned to God and come under the direct rule of "David my servant" (v.24). From this verse, 24, to the end of the chapter we are given the wonderful prospect of a life of peace and righteousness under Christ's rule. The land which Israel forfeited when she broke her covenant relationship with God shall be returned to her possession with Jerusalem once again the seat of government of the kingdom (v.25).

This parable and its prophetic message completes an over-all picture of the history and destiny of Israel, to which the previous parables in this study have also contributed. Each one covers a particular aspect of the nation's history consequent on their disobedience to God, and the resolution of the situation which ends in their eventual reinstatement as His people.

Chapter 7

The Sower

In the parables of the Old Testament the recurrent theme throughout that book is one of reconciliation between God and Israel with the promise of a future restoration to become once again His people.

Coming to the parables of the New Testament the theme reaches its conclusion, for the means of that reconciliation has become a reality in the person of our Lord, Jesus Christ, Whose sacrifice will free Israel from the bond of the old Covenant as foreshadowed in the parable of *Hosea*. By Christ's sacrifice the kingdom is redeemed, i.e. the redemption price for the breaking of the old Covenant, which is death, has been paid. The need for this ultimate sanction is referred to by the apostle Paul when he declares that "...the wages of sin is death." (*Romans* ch.6 v.23). Redemption, then, clears the way for the restoration of the kingdom. It clears the way, also, for the restoration of all creation from its fallen state, of which the account is given in the 3rd chapter of *Genesis*.

However, in the progression to that eventual state of universal accord with God, His kingdom must first be restored to a perfected state so that it can be a sure witness to the omnipotence and omnipresence of God our Creator. The rest of mankind will then have the opportunity to become citizens of the kingdom by accepting Christ as their Saviour, Lord and King.

But that is still in the future for the kingdom has not yet repented of her evil ways and turned back to God. At the time of our Lord's first advent the people of Israel were, in fact, still scattered abroad. St. James acknowledges this at the time when he addresses his epistle to: "...the twelve tribes scattered abroad." Therefore the news of their redemption has to be taken to them and that is the commission given by Jesus to the apostles: "...go rather to the lost sheep of the house of Israel." (*Matthew* ch.10 v.6)

The Jews in those days were only a small remnant of the people of Israel, being mainly the descendants of the tribes of Judah and Benjamin. Judea was a province of the Roman Empire and under the jurisdiction of a Roman procurator. Through their misinterpretation of the Scriptures the Jews were expecting the coming of one who would be their king and restore their independence. When Christ came in His role as the Messiah they would not accept Him. At His trial before Pilate the prospect of His release from custody was rejected by the people, who made known their own preference; "Not this man, but Barabbas."

However, there were those in Galilee whom the Lord found receptive to His teaching and from amongst them He chose His disciples. The Galileans were descendants of the tribe of Benjamin, the tribe which, at the division of the kingdom after Solomon's reign, God decreed would remain with the House of Judah (I *Kings* ch.11). In them a part of the nation would remain which was loyal to the dynasty of king David, still represented in the House of Judah until Christ's first advent.

Our Lord's discourses to the Jews included the parables which, as will be seen, are word pictures illustrating future situations in the life of the kingdom. The disciples asked Him why He told the people stories without disclosing to them the true meaning. His reply was:

"Because it is given unto you to know the mysteries of the kingdom of heaven but to them it is not given."

The hostile attitude of the Jews to our Lord's teaching and their misinterpretation of the prophecies concerning the advent of the Messiah would be a bar to their understanding of the message of the parables. So, to the disciples He gave the meaning behind the illustrations but to the mass of people who heard His words He gave no such light.

He states further His reason for withholding from them the true meaning of the parables when He declared:

"Therefore I speak to them in parables; because they seeing see not, and hearing hear not, neither do they understand." (*Matthew* ch.13 v.13)

They saw Jesus as a man, they would not see Him as the Son of God. They heard His teaching but it ran counter to their beliefs and traditions so they could not understand His meaning.

In these parables of the New Testament gospels there is a recurrent theme also, for they, too, are prophetic in their scope. The apostles knew that our Lord's death and resurrection would provide the means of reconciliation and the implication for the kingdom was surely realised, also, as can be seen from the question they put to the risen Lord:

"Will thou at this time restore again the kingdom to Israel?"

Restoration of the kingdom was frequently contained in the message of the prophets to Israel, however severe the condemnation for her misdeeds preceding the promise. Hence we see restoration being the predominant theme in the New Testament parables, for they give insights into developments in the kingdom in the latter days right up to the end of the age.

The first of these parables is given in the 13th chapter of the gospel of *Matthew*. The writer sets the scene of one particular incident in which a large crowd of people gather to hear Jesus, who addresses them as they assemble on the shore. He boards a boat from which vantage point He can be more easily heard.

He begins by relating the parable of the sower, one familiar to all Christians. The seed falls on different types of ground with differing results, as the first nine verses relate. The interpretation is given but not to the crowd, only to the disciples as we see when we read on.

It is generally believed that this parable is a description of the varying degree of receptiveness of people to the Christian gospel down through the ages. Many hear it but reject it out of hand; amongst others the receptiveness varies from the lukewarm to the whole-hearted acceptance of the Lord. In spiritual terms the harvest varies in quantity and quality.

This interpretation is obviously valid as we know from the history of our national faith demonstrated, as it is, in church life down through the centuries to the present day. But the message of the parable is not confined to the spiritual dimension alone.

What is the seed? In our Lord's words in verse 19 it is the "word of the kingdom." It is God's word concerning the kingdom: it is the gospel or good news of the kingdom.

The Jews of His day regarded themselves as the nucleus of the kingdom for they were still resident in the promised land and retained a formal observance of the old Mosaic laws and retained their identity. Yet, for their rejection of the Messiah, Jesus prophesied their coming judgement in these words:

"The kingdom of God will be taken from you and given to a *nation* bringing forth the fruits thereof" (*Matthew* ch.21 v.43).

The 'nation' (Gk. *ethnos*) our Lord referred to could only be Israel in the 'appointed place,' with the 'fruits' brought forth being the produce of that gospel message which was to be spread world-wide from Britain's island sanctuary.

We have little, if any, knowledge of how well the kingdom message was received by our ancestors back in the 1st century A.D.. Perhaps, as we find today, Paul found even in his time that knowledge of their Israel identity had become lost when he caught up with the scattered tribes who had reached western Europe. He apparently knew this would be the case for he said in his letter to the Romans: "...blindness in part is happened to Israel."

The implication of that statement has proved to be accurate for, down the centuries, historical evidence shows that there have always been groups and individuals who have known of the nation's ancestral roots set in biblical history. At the beginning of this century the kingdom identity teaching was comparatively well received and accepted in Britain and in the Commonwealth. But, as with the spiritual dimension of Christian belief, so also is this belief in the kingdom of God on earth receiving fewer adherents in these last days of this age. Like the reception given to the preaching of the Christian church the preaching of the kingdom evangel has, likewise, received a mixed reception, varying from some whole-hearted acceptance to total rejection.

In the prophecies referring to the end of this age a falling away from the faith was one of the signs we were to see prior to our Lord's return. Paul in his second letter to the Thessalonians refers to this, using the Greek word *apostasia,* from which, of course, we get our English word apostasy. The weakness of the witness to the true faith today is all too apparent while apostasy abounds with the increase in materialism and moral and spiritual decay within the kingdom.

Consequences of the Mixed Reception

The very mixed results experienced by the sower in the parable have consequences which follow on from these results. These consequences can be seen in the allegorical language of the next three parables of this 13th chapter of Matthew's gospel. When studied as a whole they are found to be complementary in their significance, which will not be so obvious when each is studied in isolation, as is often done in Bible study. With this understanding in mind we come to the next parable in the series, that of the wheat and the tares.

Again the subject is the sowing of certain seeds but this time the seed represents the actual kingdom itself. In our Lord's own interpretation of the parable, given to the disciples (vs.36-43), He identifies the good seed as the children of Israel, scattered at that time in the world which is called 'the field' in the analogy. The tares, He says, are the children of the wicked one, who is Satan.

It is, perhaps, helpful to know that the tares referred to in the parable is a plant whose appearance and habit closely resembles those of the wheat. Indeed they are indistinguishable until the grain has formed and begins to ripen. Only then is the ear of the tare recognisable for it is longer than that of the wheat and, as it ripens, it turns nearly black in colour, unlike the gold of the wheat.

Satan is the author of confusion and down through the ages his disciples have been beavering away in their efforts to undermine the kingdom from within. They have had a large degree of success in both the spiritual and the political life of the nation. So much so that the Christian faith and doctrine is more fragmented and adulterated than ever before. Our laws and legal framework have been moved ever further from the Divine code laid down in Scripture. Due to such unrighteous leadership emanating from church and state there is much in thought and deed in our land which gives offence to the Almighty.

In the parable we are told that at the time of the harvest the wheat and the tares will be separated, for each, by then, will be clearly identifiable. The tares represent all that offends God and His angels will be sent to separate and remove them for destruction. This should be a warning to all in the kingdom whose deeds are evil and against the laws of God and a comfort to all who hold fast to the faith and put their trust in their Saviour and Lord. The harvest will thus be a time of cleansing so that all that is wrong in the kingdom will be rooted out and destroyed.

The message of this parable is a description of the situation which would be apparent in the kingdom in the latter days and that it would be the inevitable consequence of the reaction to the sower as given in that parable.

The complementary nature of these parables is already becoming evident. The seed having been sown the news of the kingdom redeemed was brought to the British Isles; the message was given its greatest publicity at the time of the Reformation; the kingdom identity later being propagated but apparently not receiving wide acceptance. The significance and relevance of these truths to the kingdom has never been fully appreciated.

The result of this is that man-made laws have governed the conduct of individual and national life, bringing in their train all the troubles which beset us in these last days. The Commandments of God, on which the Common Law of England was originally based, have largely been done away through present day legislation. Similarly the spiritual rebirth which came about at the Reformation has been largely dissipated by modernistic theology. The abandonment of our God-given principles has been a gradual but steady process affecting all aspects of our lives. The erosive nature of this process eats away at these principles, allowing the promotion of a multi-racial and multi-faith society, introducing into the kingdom alien cultures and religions which are anathema to God.

Our national characteristic of fair play and tolerance is being exploited in the gradual destruction of our Christian way of life. With the wrong kind of leadership and teaching which emanates from many quarters the tares are flourishing unnoticed, except by a few. This situation leads us in to the next parable where it is alluded to in the story of the mustard seed.

The seed of the parable is not the same as the seed which produces that familiar small herb one adds to a salad meal. In the Scripture it refers to a seed which will grow into a tree of about fifteen feet in height at maturity, and it will have many branches on which birds can perch. The parable is perfectly apt in its description of the kingdom which grew from that one seed which was Abraham.

From that seed has come the mature tree which is the kingdom at the present time. The lodging of the birds in the branches of the tree has been fulfilled. At first people from many parts of the world sought the benefits of our Christian principles and parliamentary form of government. Many of these people have taken instruction in scientific, medical and other subjects in our universitites and colleges and have returned to their own lands with the knowledge and skills thus acquired.

In recent years, however, several millions of alien people have come to lodge in the kingdom, making it their home and bringing with them their own particular cultures and beliefs which they continue to practise in our midst. This is permitted, even encouraged, by our authorities under the illusion that to forbid these practices would be a denial of freedom and human rights. Such is the apostasy of present day religious thought that the faith once delivered to the saints has been washed away in a veritable sea of vague, non-specific do-goodery.

The idea that our government might have obligations to protect our Christian heritage seems to have been abandoned. The idea that aliens who wish to settle in our midst have obligations regarding their need to conform to the laws and religion of the kingdom seems no longer to be considered.

The kingdom was intended to be an example to the rest of the world, an influence for good and for hope in a world ravaged by the disease of sin and death which invaded man's domain in the garden of Eden. But what sort of influence can it have on the world in its present condition? Are other nations likely to be impressed by what they see? Can they benefit by following our example today?

The next parable, the fourth and last of the group which Jesus related to the crowd, provides an answer to these questions. In this our Lord likens the kingdom to leaven, which a woman takes and hides in three measures of meal until it is completely leavened.

Firstly the words of this parable should direct our thoughts back to an important place in Scripture, *Genesis* ch.18, where the Lord, accompanied by two angels, appears to Abraham and foretells the birth of a son to his wife Sarah.

Abraham apparently recognised the Divine presence, addressing Him as "my Lord." He offers the three hospitality and then asked Sarah to get "...three measures of fine meal... and make cakes upon the hearth."

So the words of the parable are not just mere coincidence but identify the kingdom in that clear reference to its foundation in what was to be the miraculous birth of Isaac to parents long past child-bearing age.

The statement that the leaven was 'hidden' is not without some significance for, indeed, the kingdom has been hidden to the world at large in accordance with the purposes of God. As is well known leaven is a transforming agent, necessary in association with dough for making bread. Its characteristic of being able to transform and spread made it a suitable choice for its use in several biblical analogies. On other occasions commentators seem agreed that leaven is associated with things that are evil when it appears in Scripture. Certainly Paul, in his first letter to the Corinthians (ch.5), castigates them for some moral corruption he found there, likening it to leaven, for if it was not checked and the culprit punished the corruption would spread.

In *Matthew* ch.16 Jesus gives His disciples a warning:

"...beware the leaven of the Pharisees and of the Sadducees..."

The disciples thought that our Lord was referring to the bread but, seeing their misunderstanding He explains what He meant:

"Then understood they how that He bade them not beware of the leaven of the bread, but of the doctrine of the Pharisees and of the Sadducees" (v.12).

This false doctrine was condemned by Jesus for, like leaven, it could and did spread amongst the people. So, as we look at the kingdom today in its state of apostasy and unrighteousness, it will surely be obvious that its influence on the rest of the world cannot be good. Nor can it be, until it is cleansed of all those things which offend God and comes under the righteous rule of His Son, Jesus Christ.

Divine Countermeasures

The next three parables we come to may appear quite different in subject but, as they are studied, it will be found that they have a close affinity with the three previous ones. The first of these, in verse 44, is the parable of the treasure hidden in the field, "...which when a man had found it he hideth it (covered it over – *Ferrar Fenton* trans.) and buyeth the field."

Again, as our Lord stated earlier, the field is the world. The treasure is the kingdom, a description used of Israel back in the book of *Exodus* ch.19 when God said of her:

"Ye shall be a peculiar treasure unto Me."

The harmony of Scripture is again seen here in God's consistent use of words or phrases which link together different parts of Scripture. It is as though the Scriptures have their own built-in cross reference system by which its truth can be upheld.

In our Lord's first advent He came into the field, which is the world. Knowing that the treasure was hidden in this field He bought it, paying the highest price He could for it which was the giving of His own life.

The brief account given in the parable was of great prophetic significance at the time. The whole purpose of our Lord's mission was stated in these few words. His death would mean that the sins of Israel would be hidden or covered by His blood shed on Calvary and by this means also the curse of sin and death affecting all mankind would be removed.

This parable, therefore, pointed, at the time, to a milestone or turning point in the history of the kingdom and of mankind in general. It pointed to the coming fulfilment of the promise made to Abraham, many centuries before, that through his seed all the families of the earth would be blessed.

Another milestone in the history of the kingdom is marked in the next parable. In it Jesus said:

"...the kingdom of heaven is like a merchantman seeking goodly pearls; who when he had found one pearl of great price he sold all that he had and bought it."

The kingdom is likened to a merchantman so the kingdom is not the pearl of great price; neither is our Lord that pearl for He cannot be bought, He gave Himself freely for the kingdom and for all creation.

In looking for something further of great importance in the history of the kingdom we should look forward in time from Calvary. The British Isles were populated by descendants of the scattered tribes but we know that it was another thousand years before the last of these arrived and settled, recorded in this history as the Norman conquest. Though this marked the completion of the resettlement in the 'appointed place' of the dispersed people of Israel it was not a new or outstanding development in that history.

What was new and outstanding later in the history of the kingdom was the Reformation. Prior to that our nation had come through what was known as the 'dark ages,' when the spiritual life of the people was under the influence or control of the church of Rome. The printing of the Word of God in the language of the people and the preaching of the Reformed faith was an event which brought new light to a spiritually dark land. Here, surely, was the pearl of great price, the Word of God. Not just in financial terms, though certainly it could be bought for money just as it can today. But, like the previous parable, the highest price which could be paid was life itself. Such is the value that men and women placed on the Scriptures in those early days of the Protestant church, for the power of Rome was not broken just then and martyrdom for the Protestant faith was not an infrequent occurrence.

That the Word of God is such a pearl of great price is surely alluded to in our Coronation service. When the newly crowned monarch is presented with the Bible the Archbishop, in his address, refers to it as:

"...the most valuable thing this world affords..."

The Christian principles on which our national life is based are principles we have in the past fought to preserve when they were threatened by foreign powers. Thus we demonstrated the value we still placed on this pearl, and rightly so. But what value do we place on it these days? Apparently not very much, as is indicated in the third parable of this group:

"Again the kingdom of heaven is like a net that was cast into the sea and gathered of every kind; which when it was full they drew to the shore and sat down and gathered the good into vessels but cast the bad away. So shall it be at the

end of the world (age); *the angels shall come forth and sever the wicked from the just."*

With the 'sea' mentioned in the parable being analogous of the peoples of the world it will be realised that the story paints a very clear and accurate picture of the kingdom. Particularly in the past few decades there has been a gradual influx to the kingdom of foreign nationals bringing with them their different religions and cultures and contributing to the increasing state of unrighteousness within the kingdom.

In this analysis the obvious parallel with the parable of the mustard seed and the birds lodging in the tree branches will be recognised. When the net is full there is then a great sorting out to be done. This, Jesus says, is the time of the end of the age when the angels will come to separate the wicked from the just. Here, again, is another parallel situation, this one with the parable of the wheat and the tares where once more it is the angels who are sent to separate the good from the bad at the harvest.

The moral and spiritual degeneracy of the kingdom at the present time indicates the ripening state of the tares and the fullness of the net. So in expectation we await the sorting out process. This is something which we cannot do for it is beyond our human power to achieve. Only Divine power can accomplish such a task in which true justice must and will be done. It has still to take place and it will be the final milestone marking the end of an era and the beginning of the new age in the life of the kingdom. It will no longer be under man's rule and Satan's influence but under Christ's rule and God's influence, something we hope and pray will take place very soon.

With this parable we come to the end of a quite coherent message given by our Lord, notwithstanding the unusual form of its presentation. Taken as a whole it can be summarised as follows:

God is the sower proclaiming and spreading His news concerning His kingdom, but this news is not generally well received by the people. Their mixed reaction to it thus brings inevitable consequences which are described in the next three parables. These have their emphasis on the human element of the kingdom showing the effect these consequences have upon its future development. They are followed by three more parables whose emphasis is on the Divine element portraying God's contingency plans to counter the effects of the people's mixed reaction. First there is the covering of the kingdom under the blood of redemption shed on Calvary, then the injection of new spiritual life into the kingdom at the Reformation, enough to sustain it until the time of the harvest, the time of cleansing and our Lord's return in power and glory.

Thus when the parables are considered as a whole this progressive picture of the kingdom emerges, a picture which would not be apparent if each one is studied independently.

At the end of His discourse Jesus puts the question to the disciples: "Have ye understood all these things?"

At that time the only Scriptures available to the disciples were those of the Old Testament. As well as containing a history of the Israel people the prophetic parts of those writings concerned their future destiny and was better understood then by the disciples than it is by any of our learned theologians today. Their recognition of Jesus as the Son of God and the part He would play in that destiny, in accordance with prophecy would also be known and understood. They, too, would see these parables as parts of a whole message.

Hence they were able to reply to the Lord's question quite truthfully when they said: "Yes Lord."

The New and The Old of Equal Importance

He then gives them another short parable, the last one of the group, being like the concluding remarks at the end of a story:

"Then said He unto them: Therefore every scribe which is instructed into the kingdom of heaven is like unto an householder which bringeth forth out of his treasure things new and old."

Here again we see the association between the kingdom and treasure. A householder's treasure would be his most valued possession which would surely be the Word of God concerning the kingdom. That which was new concerning the kingdom in those days was undoubtedly the new Covenant of grace through faith introduced by Christ's sacrifice; the new Covenant promised through the prophet Jeremiah (ch.31). Salvation through faith in the risen Lord was new, bringing to all who professed such faith the promise of everlasting life. That which was old, yet still of infinite value and part of the treasure, are the enduring covenants and all the promises made to the patriarchs.

The scribe which is instructed into the kingdom of heaven will not take account of only that which is new or only that which is old; they are interdependent and cannot rightfully be separated. They are all part of that great treasure, the whole gospel of the kingdom.

Chapter 8

The Workers in the Vineyard

The next parable we come to is in *Matthew* chapter 20. It is given as an answer to a point raised by Peter of which we read in the previous chapter at verse 27. The disciples have just heard the Lord's reply to the young man who had asked Him how he could gain eternal life. They are then told that it is easier for a camel to go through the eye of a needle than for a rich man to enter the kingdom of God. The eye of a needle in this parable does not, of course, refer to a sewing implement nor would it be understood as such by the disciples. As they would know it referred to a small door in the city gate which was opened after dark when the main door was closed. A camel could just get through this door provided its load had first been removed. The point being made by Jesus was that the rich young man who had asked what he had to do to obtain eternal life had been told to 'unload' his wealth and give it to the poor then follow Him. This was more than he had bargained for and he went off a troubled young man.

Peter then claims that they had all given up their worldly possessions and followed the Lord and, therefore, wanted to know what they would receive by way of recompense. In v.28 Jesus states that in the new age to come when He sits upon 'the throne of His glory' the disciples would also sit upon twelve thrones judging the twelve tribes of Israel. This can be no mere spiritual situation but must be a prophetic vision of the literal kingdom of God on earth having at its head the Lord as King and the disciples as His cabinet ministers overseeing the righteous government of the kingdom. This, in answer to Peter's question, is their reward for their faith and service. Jesus follows this by saying that all who, in effect,

50

renounce worldly things that would come in the way of their true worship and service for the Lord would receive everlasting life.

The Lord then states: "But many that are first shall be last; and the last shall be first."

This is immediately followed by the parable of the workers in the vineyard. "For the kingdom of heaven is like unto a man that is an householder, which went out early in the morning to hire labourers into his vineyard."

The story goes on to relate the hiring of the workers then and at other times during the day, each group agreeing to the wage offered by the householder. At the end of the working day the labourers assembled to receive their wages and each received the same amount, one penny. Those who started early and worked through the heat of the day complained at the seeming injustice but the householder reminded them that they had agreed to the wage offered so were not being treated unfairly. The Lord then reiterates His earlier remark: "So the last shall be first and the first last; for many be called but few chosen."

The whole theme of this discourse is faith and service in the kingdom. The time is the Christian era and up to the beginning of the age under Christ's rule. The disciples' reward for their faith and service was promised to them, being those positions of authority in the kingdom in the new age. All who throughout the Christian era made the things of this world subordinate to the true faith and worship of the Lord would receive everlasting life.

As we know there are many different religious groups in the land who profess their belief in Christ and His teaching. They cannot all be exponents of the true faith and many will come under the condemnation of the Lord Whose reply to their cry of "Lord, Lord" will be: "I never knew you; depart from Me..." (*Matthew* ch.7 v.21-23)

In *Matthew* ch.5 v.19 it is made clear that those who disobey the laws of God and who teach men so to do will be counted as least in the kingdom, but those who observe to do them shall be called the greatest in the kingdom. Thus our position in the kingdom is dependent on our observance of God's commandments, statutes and judgements in our individual and national life. Orthodox Christian teaching has caused much needless confusion in its bald declaration: 'We are not under law but under grace.' As the statement stands it is a direct contradiction of the Lord's words referred to in *Matthew* ch.5. The statement is only true when it is made with respect to the law contained in the ordinances of the Old Testament which dealt solely with the offerings and sacrifices to be made by the people. It was only these which were terminated by our Lord's death on Calvary.

Many who profess their faith and obedience to Christ pay mere lip service to His commandments. Their faith is without works, i.e. they are ignorant of the will of God declared through His righteous laws and thus their way of life is centred on the purely spiritual aspect of that faith. So, in the words of Scripture, it is a dead faith. They are among the many who receive Christ's call to be with Him in His kingdom but will not be chosen to hold positions of influence and responsibility. They will be the least in the kingdom as is declared in the gospel. The few who are 'chosen' are those who will be placed in positions of authority in the kingdom, being referred to as 'greatest in the kingdom.' This is not favouritism or class distinction as we might think of it, it is the just recompense of the Lord for faith and obedience to Him. God is our Judge and trusting in His fairness in His judgements one can be sure that citizenship in His kingdom will be a privilege and a blessing whether one is regarded as least or greatest.

Many have gone before us in the past few hundred years and have suffered in various ways for their faith, labouring through 'the heat of the day.' In spite of that they are no more worthy of a place in the kingdom than those who at the present time and up till the end of the age come to a knowledge of the Lord as their Saviour and the Redeemer of Israel. Like the labourers in the vineyard the reward or payment for faithful service is the same for all.

The few that are 'chosen' may be distinguishable from the 'many called' by their recognition of the fulfilment of prophecy in the literal earthly kingdom of a covenant-keeping God. Even at this late time of this age those who come to such a knowledge and belief will be the 'last' yet will precede those of previous generations who, though first to proclaim their faith in Christ crucified, did not embrace the full gospel of the kingdom of God in the restored nation of Israel.

While citizenship of the kingdom is open to non-Israel peoples the laws concerning the status of the alien in Israel, recorded in the Old Testament Scriptures, will still be in force. Under these laws the alien is restricted in his influence and authority within the kingdom and obliged to observe the laws of the land and worship only the one true God. There is no provision in the kingdom of God for a multi-faith society. With the restrictions imposed by the law on aliens it is clear that they will not be among the 'chosen few' who will be leaders in the kingdom in the new age. This will no doubt go against all the modern racial integrationists and racial equality devotees proclaim. However, the faults and failings these people see in our society will only be compounded by the actions they advocate for they are contrary to the laws of God. It will be this Divine code of law which will operate in the kingdom when Christ returns as King over Israel. The benefits which will accrue from their compliance will be enjoyed by every citizen in the kingdom, a situation which will become the envy of other nations, as is foretold by the prophet Micah (ch.4 vs.1-2).

This prophecy of *Micah* refers to the new kingdom age under Christ's rule when the blessings of His government will be clearly demonstrated in the life of the nation. It will thus fulfil its destiny of being the example for all nations to follow that they, too, might come to the Lord and accept Him as King of kings and Lord of lords.

Chapter 9

The Hidden Treasure

In Mark's gospel, chapter 4, we read again the parable of the Sower which is the same as that given in Matthew's gospel. However, the agrarian theme is pursued a little further by Jesus as is given in verses 26-29 by the writer. The kingdom is like seed which has been cast into the ground. The man who has cast it watches day by day for it to shoot forth from the ground; first the blade then the ear and finally the full grown corn.

The miraculous growth of the plant from the seed, which has been hidden from view in the ground for a time until germination and first growth has taken place, describes the development of the kingdom. After their removal from the promised land and their captivity in Assyria the kingdom was hidden from the eyes of the world. Like a seed God planted them in a new location where they remained hidden.

When one plants a seed in the ground one merely watches to see its progress, having no part in the growth process. It already has within it that spark of life and is dependent on God, the giver of all life, for its growth and development. So also is the kingdom, which makes the analogy so very appropriate.

When the kingdom seed germinated and began to grow its identity was not recognised by the world at large. The peoples of the British Isles were just another nation among nations. But to God the developing plant was something special and throughout its growth He has nurtured it, protecting it against all the storms of life so that it would survive, blossom and bear fruit. In the parable our Lord relates that when the fruit appears the sickle is immediately brought out for it is the time to harvest. Thus this parable, too, brings us to the end of the age.

The harvesting of many crops can be a fairly critical time. Gather it in too soon and the crop will not be at its best or may even be unfit to use. Do it too late and the result will be the same. So, too, will be the time of the harvest at the end of the age. We are not in a position to know the day or time when the kingdom will be right for God's harvest. We are given glimpses through the prophecies of Scripture of the conditions to be expected at that critical time, but the day or hour even the Lord Himself did not know.

When we look at the state of the kingdom at the present time we may well despair of it ever being suitable to serve God's purpose. Yet through the words of prophecy we know that the state of the kingdom will not be judged by human standards when God judges it to be ready for the harvest. From Scripture we learn that the people of Israel in the Isles will, in these last days of the age, be driven by force of circumstances to turn from their unrighteous way and seek God's help. A critical time indeed. If God were to act before that time we would not be in the right frame of mind or spirit to recognise His hand and as a crop we would not be usable. If He delays in answering our call the crop would quickly wither and die. That such a possibility exists is clearly affirmed by the words of our Lord recorded in *Matthew* ch.24: "except these days be shortened there should no flesh be saved; But for the elect's sake these days shall be shortened."

The serious situation facing the kingdom at the end of the age is reflected in the unmistakable sense of urgency with which the short parable ends: "...*immediately* he putteth in the sickle..."

Timing is therefore all-important. However, as has been pointed out already we are in God's hands and His timing will ensure that the harvest will take place at exactly the right moment.

56

Chapter 10

The Two Sons

Returning to Matthew's gospel there are a further three parables which can be seen to be related, there being a continuity in their subject matter. In chapter 21 vs. 28-32, there is first the parable of the two sons, being, in a way, like an introduction to the two parables which follow it.

Each son is approached by their father and asked to go and work in the vineyard. The first son refuses to go but later relented and did as he was asked. The second son agreed to his father's request but then did not carry it out. Jesus asks His listeners which son they thought had carried out the wishes of their father and they reply that it was the first son. Jesus was in the temple at the time and addressing the chief priests and elders. They had already rejected the call of John the Baptist and our Lord now tells them that publicans and harlots, the lowest form of human life in Jewish eyes, would precede them into the kingdom.

In this parable the two sons represent the two houses of Israel and Judah. The first son who refused to do his father's bidding but then relented represents the house of Israel. The simple analogy highlights one aspect of the history of that people. They rejected the laws and authority of God and for hundreds of years were dispersed among the nations before settling in the British Isles. But, after settling there, the gospels of Redemption and Salvation were brought to the people and the Christian church and faith was established in the kingdom. The word of God came into print and the Christian gospel was preached abroad. In this spiritual revival and awakening we see the change of heart symbolically illustrated by the first son who had second thoughts.

A section of the house of Judah, on the other hand, remained in the vicinity of their own land and returned, in part, to it thus maintaining a representation of the kingdom in its former territory with Jerusalem still as its centre. However, this chance to uphold the laws and authority of God was not grasped. Their misuse of their privileged position was condemned by our Lord on many occasions. On one of these He said: "Thus have ye made the commandments of God of none effect by your tradition." (*Matthew* ch.15 v.6). Then he quotes from *Isaiah:* "This people draw nigh unto Me with their mouth and honoureth Me with their lips, but their heart is far from Me. But in vain do they worship Me, teaching for doctrines the commandments of men" (vs. 8-9).

This short parable is like a character study showing the difference in attitude of the two sons, which reflected those of the two kingdoms they represented. The house of Israel came to accept Christ as the Son of God, Saviour and Redeemer, and the Scriptures as the written Word of God. The Jews have never accepted Christ as the Son of God and their Talmud is a version of the Scriptures with their own religious traditions included therein. Their worship is thus invalidated in God's eyes.

In the next parable a vineyard is again the setting for the story. The second son of the previous parable is not mentioned but having established his identity with the house of Judah the story which follows depicts his actions and the consequences due to his disobedience to the father.

The Treacherous Husbandmen

The story this time is of a householder who planted a vineyard, hedged it all round, made a winepress and built a tower in the vineyard. He then let it out to husbandmen and left it in their care while he went away. When the fruit was ready for harvesting the householder sent his servants to collect it but the husbandmen beat one, killed another and stoned another. He therefore sent more servants the second time but they were treated in like manner as the first. Then he sent his son, expecting him to be shown more respect. But the husbandmen killed him too, and plotted to seize his inheritance.

Jesus asked the people what they thought the householder would do in the circumstances. They replied that he would "miserably destroy these wicked men" and let out his vineyard to other husbandmen who would give him the fruits in due season.

Our Lord then quotes from *Psalm* 118: "The stone which the builders rejected the same is become the head of the corner; this is the Lord's doing and it is marvellous in our eyes." Following this Jesus said (quoted elsewhere in this study) "The kingdom of God shall be taken from you and given to a nation bringing forth the fruits thereof." He then declared that whomsoever fell on the stone would be broken and whomsoever it fell upon would be ground to powder.

Again those hearing the parable were the chief priests and the Pharisees who, by then, recognised that the Lord was in fact referring to them.

The scene set in the first part of this parable shows the salient features of the kingdom of Israel. The householder is God who created the kingdom, which is the vineyard, placing it in the promised land and hedged around by His protective care. The winepress represented the ordinances relating to the sacrifices which had to be made in atonement for the sins of the people. These, of course, were merely forerunners to the supreme sacrifice made by our Lord, prophesied in *Isaiah* ch.63 v.3 where the same symbolism is used: i.e. "I have trodden the winepress alone."

The tower that was built was a watch tower, a type normally built to house shepherds who had flocks to protect or for watchmen who had oversight of the vineyard. Thus in the analogy it refers to the seat of government and authority which had oversight of the interests and wellbeing of the kingdom as its main function.

This parable is a repetition of the same analogy given by the prophet Isaiah in ch.5 vs.1-2. The situation described there resulted in the condemnation of the people of Judah who had failed to uphold the laws of God, signified by the wild grapes they had produced. At that time the northern house of Israel had gone into captivity and the prophet warned of the same fate to befall Judah.

Needless to say the prophets were not popular with the people when they pronounced God's judgements on them for their unrighteous behaviour. Therefore, as our Lord related in the parable, they were often badly treated. In the 23rd chapter of Matthew's gospel Jesus names the prophet Zechariah as one (servant) who had been killed.

The house of Judah was represented in our Lord's time by Idumean Jews and the descendants of the people who had returned from the Babylonian captivity in Jerusalem. In quoting from *Psalm* 118 He confirmed that the prophetic statement it contained was going to be fulfilled by His own death at the instigation of the Jews; for He was the stone which was about to be rejected. His resurrection, however, was also foretold in the same verse for, again, the same stone was to become the head corner stone. That this corner stone refers to Jesus Christ is confirmed by St. Paul in his letter to the Ephesians – "...Jesus Christ Himself being the chief corner stone" (ch.2 v.20).

Paul is referring in this part of his letter to the structure of the kingdom. To illustrate this structure in a geometric form the most appropriate figure is a pyramid. Thus Christ is the head or chief corner stone at the top of the figure. Such a stone is both the head stone and the chief corner stone for it joins at its apex the four corners of the figure. Our Lord's choice of analogy is most apt as becomes apparent. In descending order of seniority in the kingdom there are the apostles and prophets under Christ the King. Then come the leaders of the church and state and under them are the citizens of the kingdom.

If one thinks of this structure in terms of gravitational pull, which is downwards, the pyramid would seem a most inappropriate figure to use. However, if we think of our Lord's words given in John's gospel ch.12: "I, if I be lifted up from the earth, will draw all men unto Me," in spiritual terms the order given is then as we would expect, with Christ at the head exerting His spiritual attraction and upward pull.

In considering this edifice of the pyramid as being analogous of the kingdom, with Christ Himself as the chief corner stone, its stability in the physical as well as spiritual sense will be seen to be considerable. Thus our Lord's declaration that anyone falling upon it would be broken and that if it were to fall on anyone they would be ground to powder can be easily understood. History confirms that since the kingdom became re-established in the British Isles all who have tried to "fall upon" it have been defeated, a fulfilment of our Lord's prophetic statement and promise.

The Jews were destroyed as a people in A.D.70, the just reward for their misdeeds which, unwittingly, the priests and Pharisees declared would be the just reward for the wicked husbandmen. Their cry of: "His blood be upon us and on our children." was, again unwittingly, the most severe self-condemnation which could be uttered and it was fulfilled by Divine retribution. The "other husbandmen" who would render fruits in their season was, therefore, the other nation to whom the kingdom would be given.

After declaring that the stone would become "the head of the corner" the verse continues: "...this is the Lord's doing and it is marvellous in our eyes." This verse makes an important declaration which might escape notice. In John's gospel, ch.10, Jesus explains His role as the good shepherd who will lay down his life for his sheep. In vs. 17 and 18 we read:

> *"I lay down My life that I might take it again. No man taketh it from Me, but I lay it down of Myself. I have power to lay it down and I have power to take it again."*

In Israel there occurred, once each year, the sacrifice of a spotless lamb for the sins of the nation. It was carried out only by the High Priest on that occasion. While in John's gospel Christ illustrated His close association to His people as a shepherd to his flock we now come to the significance of His death as the ultimate compliance with the law of Ordinance regarding sacrifice for sin. Thus it was that Christ took upon Himself the sins of the people as the sinless or spotless lamb of sacrifice. At the same time, by the authority of the Father, He was the High Priest, not of the human Aaronic order of priests who held this office up to this point, but of the Divine order of Melchisedek (*Hebrews* ch.5 vs.5-6). His sacrificial death could not be at the hand of any human priest for none had such authority in this final forfeiture of life in atonement for sin.

The Jews were instrumental in having our Lord placed on the cross but neither they nor the Romans actually brought His life to an end. It was not in the plan of God that they should do so. In Luke's gospel, ch.23 v.46, we read His final words: "Father into Thy hand I commend My spirit, and having said thus He gave up the ghost."

How significant, then, were the words of the Psalmist – "...this is the Lord's doing (NOT man's) and it is marvellous in our eyes." It must surely have been marvellous to the disciples when He rose from the grave and came to them and "...opened their understanding that they might understand the

Scriptures." (*Luke* ch.24 v.45). Jesus goes on in the next verse: "Thus it is written and thus it behoved Christ to suffer and to rise from the dead the third day." He rose again to become "the head of the corner," the chief corner stone.

In *Matthew* ch.26, immediately following the Last Supper where the significance of the bread and the wine is revealed to the disciples, Jesus says to them: "...I will not drink henceforth of this fruit of the vine until that day when I drink it new with you in My Father's kingdom." Here again is confirmation of the symbolism of the winepress in the parable showing its association with sacrifice and the shedding of our Lord's blood. There is also in that statement the affirmation that Christ will return in His resurrection body to this earth, a prophecy which is given in many other places in Scripture and which will surely be fulfilled very soon. There is no justification for the belief that this will be a purely spiritual return of the Lord. That His spiritual presence amongst all believers is a very real experience has been so throughout the Christian era. Such a guiding presence was promised from the beginning of that era but it has always been distinct from the promise of His physical return in power and glory at the end of the age to take His rightful place on "the throne of His father David."

The Marriage of the King's Son

The third parable of this group continues the Lord's discourse in the temple to the priests and Pharisees. Having first contrasted the characters of the two houses of Israel and Judah and then followed the development of Judah and their attitude to their position of stewardship of the kingdom up to Christ's death, this third parable looks beyond that time and, once again, brings us up to the end of the age. It is contained in the first fourteen verses of chapter 22 in Matthew's gospel.

The characterisation in the analogy is, again, different as we read that the kingdom of heaven is like a king who has arranged a marriage for his son. The king's servants were sent to call the people to come to the wedding but they would not come. Other servants were then sent to the people with the message that the meal was prepared, oxen and fattened beasts killed and all preparations completed and they were bidden to attend. But the people, however, treated the servants spitefully and killed some of them. The king heard about this and in his anger he destroyed the murderers and burned down the city.

Then the king told his servants that the people had not been worthy so they were to go into the highways and extend the invitation to others, as many as they could find. This they did, gathering both bad and good, so the wedding guests were duly assembled. Amongst them was one found not to be suitably attired and his right to be there was challenged. The king ordered this person to be bound and cast into "outer darkness" and concludes "For many are called but few are chosen."

This theme of marriage should take our minds back to the parable of Hosea in which there is the promise to Israel of her future remarriage – ...thou shalt call Me Ishi" – my husband (*Hosea* ch.2 v.16). The first servants sent to the people were the prophets who foretold the events which would occur in the development of the kingdom. But the people would not listen to them, persisting instead in their own practices and beliefs. The second group of servants brought news of the killing of the oxen and fattened beasts and of the meal which was prepared and all things being ready for the great occasion.

The killing of the beast and all the necessary preparations referred to are symbolic of our Lord's sacrifice and of His Grace and His forgiveness to all who profess their faith in

Him. This was the message proclaimed by the apostles after Christ's resurrection, they being the second group of servants to convey the wedding invitation. However, their message was spurned and they suffered persecution and death at the hands of the Jews. This action brought upon the latter the wrath of God and as a kingdom they were destroyed and the Holy City burned to the ground.

As instructed, the apostles sought out the dispersed peoples of Israel, the bad as well as the good, and issued the same invitation to them. The acceptance and proclamation of the Christian gospel of repentance and faith in Christ crucified and risen again results in the wedding being attended by many guests.

The reference to the 'bad and the good' is similar in description to that used in the parable of the drag-net (*Matthew* ch.13) typifying the moral and spiritual state of the kingdom in the latter days. That the invitation is extended to the bad as well as the good is consistent with the patience and mercy of God expressed in *Ezekiel* ch.33 v.11: "I have no pleasure in the death of the wicked; but that the wicked turn from his way and live." Also, in the second epistle of Peter, ch.3, the same sentiment is expressed by the apostle: "The Lord...is longsuffering to usward, not willing that any should perish, but that all should come to repentance."

With this evidence of God's merciful disposition towards His people we can understand why the 'bad' have been included in the invitation to the marriage. They have the chance to hear the gospel of the kingdom, to then turn from their unrighteous ways and become eligible to attend the wedding ceremony.

The Greek word translated here as 'bad' is one of several words used to describe a form of evil. In this instance it appears to denote a lawless state as a result of ignorance rather than being lawless by nature which would be a more difficult condition to change. The other words refer to a state of depravity, of being just bad by nature; to lawlessness due to outright contempt for the law.

However, we know from the parables of the wheat and the tares and the drag-net that the kingdom will contain many who are unresponsive to this wedding invitation and will be cast out in the cleansing process at the end of the age. In contrast 'the good' are surely those whose hearts and minds are open to receive the gospel of the kingdom and who order their lives in accordance with this knowledge and the obligation it entails.

We then read that a certain man is found among the wedding guests who is improperly dressed. In the material sense a garment is that which, apart from providing comfort, hides our physical nakedness. In the symbology of the parable the garment referred to is that which hides a spiritual nakedness and is the garment or clothing of righteousness which is the righteousness of Christ and which covers the inherent sin of the believer. This man was not a true believer or he would not have been challenged. That he had nothing to say in his own defence was in effect a recognition and admission of his guilt when confronted with the truth. The king then orders him to be bound hand and foot and cast into outer darkness. This is followed by the statement: "...there shall be weeping and gnashing of teeth." Again there is a similarity of situation here when compared with that of the parable of the wheat and tares, which closes with virtually the same statement: "...there shall be wailing and gnashing of teeth."

Such anguish of spirit must surely stem from the remorse and frustration felt by all who are expelled from the kingdom for their failure to accept our Lord's Divinity and His position as Saviour and Redeemer of Israel. The furnace of fire to which the tares are consigned and the outer darkness referred to in this parable are symbolic of Divine judgement. God's judgement will undoubtedly be in accordance with His own law which, as the Psalmist says, is perfect and thus needs no alteration just to fit changing human attitudes and situations. One can expect, therefore, that in the cleansing process to come all whose deeds warrant the penalty of death will receive that penalty. Many others will be excluded from the kingdom until they have a change of heart and come to the Lord in faith.

The man who gatecrashes the wedding is addressed as 'Friend.' As he is not a true believer there may be some irony seen in such a greeting. When Judas betrayed the Lord with a kiss Jesus addressed him, too, as Friend which may also seem ironic in the circumstances. However, as some Bible students believe, this may be an example of our Lord's compassion knowing that Judas would shortly end his own life after the betrayal.

The Greek word which is translated as 'friend' in these two instances and in one other (in the parable of the workers in the vineyard) denotes a family or racial relationship rather than a social or spiritual affinity. It would, therefore, be consistent with the statement made by John the Baptist during his ministry when he told the Jews that their descent from Abraham did not absolve them from the need for repentance. Likewise today our racial descent as Israelites does not mean that we have no need of repentance and forgiveness through the blood of our Lord shed for us on Calvary. Our admission to the marriage feast will be dependent on us being suitable clothed. This is borne out in the final statement with which the parable ends: "For many are called but few are chosen." a repetition of the words with which the parable of the workers in the vineyard also ends.

The linking of these three parables contained in *Matthew* ch.21 and 22 contrasts the temperaments of the two sons, primarily portraying the main characteristic of the house of Judah and the resulting judgement which befell her. It was a fulfilment of the condemnation given in earlier times by the prophet Jeremiah through whom God said: "The backsliding Israel hath justified herself more than treacherous Judah." (ch.3 v.11). The previous few verses of that chapter describe the characteristics of the two kingdoms which God compares, showing Judah, by her treachery, to come out worse in His judgement. Israel, however, as is clearly shown, also had her faults and would not escape judgement.

Chapter 11

The Prodigal Son

The analogy of two sons illustrating historically the lives of the two kingdoms appears again in St. Luke's gospel (ch.15) in the parable generally known by the title – The Prodigal Son. In contrast to the two previous parables this one deals mainly with the house of Israel, giving a brief outline of her history, from her birth as a separate kingdom under Jeroboam, up to the end of the age, a period of nearly 2,900 years.

This parable relates the story of a man and his two sons, the younger of whom asks to be given his share of the family inheritance and then leaves home. He travels to a far country where he spends his substance in riotous living. The parable goes on to relate that there was then a great famine in the land and the son began to be in want. He then joins himself to another citizen who sends him into the fields to feed swine. The son was then in such a low state that he would have eaten the husks that the swine ate but no one gave him anything. He comes to his senses and thinks of the abundance of food back at home and decides to return to his father, confess that he has done wrong and is willing to be just a servant. However, his father sees him coming and prepares to welcome him home. The elder brother questions the justification for this welcome celebration but is told that his younger brother had been lost and presumed dead and, therefore, his return was worthy of celebration. He was reminded that he had always been with his father, had never been lost and that his share of the inheritance was still there for him.

The departure of the younger son is analogous of the division of the kingdom after Solomon's reign and the creation of the northern ten-tribed kingdom of Israel under the leadership of Jeroboam. The journeying to a far country illustrates briefly that period of time during which that people are dispersed, first into captivity in Assyria, then in their westward migration to their settlement in the British Isles. Over the centuries the material wealth of the kingdom increased as colonial expansion took place and industry and commerce increased. The spiritual wealth of the kingdom also blossomed at the time of the Reformation which brought a period of blessing to the nation. Thus, Britain became the commercial centre of the world and through the spreading of the Word of God world-wide, was an influence for good in a dark age.

But the son, we are told, spent his substance in riotous living. That expression may conjure up in our mind a vision of a dissolute or frivolous lifestyle, which would be serious enough. However, riotous in the context of the parable should be regarded more specifically as being lawless and, in this case, meaning that his way of life was contrary to the laws of God. This describes very accurately the situation we have seen developing in the Israel nations over the years, particularly in recent times. In the last three hundred years business and commercial activities have become tied to financial system which have imposed an increasing burden of debt on both individuals and on the nations as a whole. Such a system is against Divine economics and causes needless hardship and suffering. Getting into debt was a situation which the law recognised some people might have to face but, for the protection of their quality of life, such debts were limited in their duration to a maximum of seven years. On such debts the imposition of interest charges, or usury, was not permitted. If the debt had not been fully repaid by the end of the seven year period what was still owing was cancelled. Likewise the national debt was not allowed to go on for more than forty-nine years. Every 50th year in the life of the kingdom was the Jubilee year when all debts were released. A study of the Divine Law reveals that the wellbeing of every individual and the prosperity of the kingdom as a whole was guaranteed when it was obeyed (*Deuteronomy* ch.28 vs.1-14).

In the field of politics, at both local and national levels, man-made laws have replaced the righteous laws of God. Hence true justice and equity is not enjoyed by the people, resulting in a diminishing of loyalty and respect in the nation for government and authority.

The Reformation brought about a great spiritual revival in the land raising moral and spiritual values for a time in the nation. But even this spiritual wealth has been wasted, for false doctrines and false teaching have crept into our places of worship and learning. Modernists in their, so-called, enlightenment have produced their own interpretations of the Scriptures in which they deny the virgin birth of our Lord, deny His bodily resurrection and deny His sinless nature. In their denial of these fundamental truths, their rejection of the authenticity of much of the Holy Bible and the spiritualising of many parts of it, the spiritual wealth of the nations has also been riotously, or lawlessly, thrown away.

In St. Paul's second letter to the Thessalonians he refers in the second chapter to a period in which there will be a 'falling away.' The Greek word so translated is *apostasia,* from which, of course, we get the word apostasy. Our Lord undoubtedly knew of this apostasy in our day, a sign of His imminent return in power; for in St. Luke's gospel, in the 18th chapter, He declares in the form of a question: "...when the Son of man cometh, shall He find faith on the earth?"

The translators of the New Testament did not always include the definite article in their translation from the original Greek text, no doubt thinking it was superfluous in many places. However, these omissions sometimes altered the sense of a passage or statement as has been done in the verse just quoted. Thus it should read: "...shall He find *the* faith on the earth?" There are many millions who profess *a* faith but apparently few who profess *the* faith.

Turning again to the parable it goes on to state that there was then a great famine in the land and the son began to be in want. Looking around us we do not see any signs of the nations being short of food. Also, as the sequence of events related in the parable is studied, it is seen that after the coming of this famine the son goes and joins himself to a citizen of the land. If the famine does not refer at this time to a food shortage there must be some other explanation to be found.

The meaning becomes apparent when we turn to the prophecy of Amos where, in the 8th chapter and at v.11, God declares:

"Behold the days come, saith the Lord God, that I will send a famine in the land, not a famine of bread, nor a thirst for water, but of hearing the words of the Lord."

This meaning of the word will be seen to be most appropriate to these days in which we live. There is, indeed, a great famine of the word of God in the nations and the consequences of this famine are manifest in the many troubles we now face.

Considering Britain in particular, in the material sense we still seem outwardly to be a fairly prosperous nation. But economic and financial problems have been getting steadily worse since the last war, in spite of the various measures successive governments have introduced. The great solution to these troubles was to be Britain's entry into the E.E.C., so we were told. Certainly, membership of this group of nations, by acceptance of the Treaty of Rome, is the most significant milestone in Britain's modern history.

When, in the parable, the son joined himself to this other citizen it will be found that the word in the original Greek text which has been translated as 'joined' means, literally, to glue together, a very permanent union. According to the *Companion Bible* notes the sense of the wording in this passage imply that the son forced himself into the company of this other person. This is very descriptive of the way our political leaders of the day forced our entry into the European Community in spite of the initial rebuffs received from General de Gaulle. This union, which at first was said to be purely economic with no loss of sovereignty involved, has clearly become a political union also, however much our political leaders deny such an intention.

The son seemed to be fairly securely tied to the other citizen and suffered much degradation in being sent to feed the swine. We have suffered the humiliation of seeing surplus food we have helped to produce being sold off cheaply to the Russians. We seem to be importing many things which we are quite capable of producing ourselves and thus depriving some of our own citizens of the opportunity to make a living. The feeding of swine was considered the meanest of tasks and thus typifies the state of servility we seem to be coming to as our government's power becomes increasingly subordinate to the European Parliament.

The parable goes on to relate the plight of the son who now suffers from shortage of food and feeling that he could even eat the husks, the pods of the carob tree, which were fed to the swine. This situation is different to the famine mentioned earlier and in the sequence of events this indicates a time when Israel is under threat from hostile powers at the end of this age. The 38th and 39th chapters of *Ezekiel* refer to such powers which come to prominence at this time and Bible students mostly agree that Gog, Magog, Meshech and Tubal named there are synonymous with Russia and her neighbours. Whether this hostility reaches its zenith in the federalist one-world and anti-kingdom ideology, which is opposed to the nation state, or in the spreading of Muslim fundamentalism, a potent force now emerging in Eastern Europe and patently anti-Christian, remains to be seen. The certainty is that the threat will come from that racial descendancy, for the ancestry of these European and Russian peoples goes back to earlier nations who were enemies of ancient Israel.

In the parable the son is brought to his senses by his predicament and remembers the better times he enjoyed at home with his father. So, the story relates, he simply rose and returned home. There is, it seems, no protest from the citizen to whom he was joined, no obstacle appears to be in his way, he is apparently free to return home.

However deeply we become committed to the European Union some serious political or ideological upheaval on that continent could very well bring that alliance to an end and free us of this modern bondage. We would be on our own, humanly speaking, once again facing an enemy across the English Channel. The situation throughout the world will be such that we will have no cause to hope for help from any quarter:

"...and no man gave unto him" (v.16).

The seriousness of our plight will be such that the kingdom will be brought to its sense and to its knees. As the son returns to his father in a repentant frame of mind so, too, will Israel turn back to God as her only refuge and help. Then, like the father seeing his son coming home, God will see the change of heart in Israel and while she is approaching Him in prayer He will be answering her need.

The climax of this age will be a time of frustration and despair as people come to the realisation of the inadequacy of their own efforts, their own methods and their own way of thinking. They will come to realise the futility of our political leadership and the falseness of our present spiritual leadership at such a time. Indeed such a realisation is, perhaps, becoming apparent in the apathy now being shown towards both these institutions. In times of national crisis in the past we have been blessed with leaders who have brought the nation successfully through those periods and for that service they have received due credit. But at the coming final crisis of this age no human leader or organisation will be equal to the task. God alone will bring order out of the man-made chaos and to Him alone will the credit and all the glory be given.

The elder brother in the parable represents the house of Judah, a portion of whom were in Judea at the time of our Lord's ministry. Known then as Jews they have never lost their identity as a people even although the kingdom was taken from them. There are to this day descendants of these people still in Palestine, an ethnic minority among many of other races who (as has already been stated) are Jews by religion rather than by racial descent. This nucleus of the house of Judah still hold to their old Talmudic tradition and still do not accept Christ to be the Messiah. For them the Messiah has yet to come. The celebration of the younger son's return home is equivalent to the marriage feast related in the previous parable in this study and is the occasion of our Lord's second advent.

While the son is being fêted his elder brother is working in the field and returns home to find the festivities in full swing. On learning the reason for it he makes known to his father his displeasure at the welcome given to his brother and refuses to join the celebration. Thus it would appear that the Jews, in Palestine and wherever they have settled, will still reject our Lord when He returns to be King over His kingdom.

The people of Judah did not reject the law or the worship of Jehovah as Israel did when the kingdom became divided in the 9th century B.C.. They preserved the oracles of God, maintained the priesthood and continued to worship in the Temple. Although this ceased during their captivity in

Babylon it was reinstated when their return from exile to Jerusalem under Ezra and Nehemiah had taken place. The Jews of our Lord's time were thus still in their ancestral home even though under Roman jurisdiction. Over the centuries Jews have continued to live in Palestine, often under difficult conditions as power positions changed during that time. A characteristic of their faith is that it has always bound them together to live in close community and this has been true wherever exiled Jews have settled in other parts of the world.

Orthodox, rabbinical Jewry have retained the Old Testament Scriptures as the focus of their teaching though coloured by their Talmudic and other writings. It can thus be seen that as a people they have never lost their identity as did the House of Israel. The fact is confirmed in the parable when the father says: "Son, thou art ever with me...," and he goes on to say: "...and all that I have is thine." The Scriptures contain all the promises of God which includes the coming of Messiah, our Saviour and Lord. Israel has accepted these promises in her declaration of Christianity as the national faith. Although in these last days of this age, apostasy is increasing, her coming change of heart and repentance will bring the appropriate response from God at a critical time.

But the Jews have no such change of heart and will still not receive Christ as their Saviour and Lord. Their inheritance is there but they will not accept it.

With this further analogy of two sons and their very different situations it can be seen that the histories of Israel and Judah are illustrated in remarkable detail in these parables.

Chapter 12

The Unworthy Steward

Christ's ministry received considerable hostility from the Jewish hierarchy and this attitude was perpetuated in the character of the Jews in the generations to follow. This would be known to the Lord and although the kingdom, i.e. the position of governmental power and authority over the people of Israel, was to be taken from them their influence in the affairs of the kingdom would still be significant. This is illustrated in a further parable in St. Luke's gospel, in chapter 16, and is known as the parable of the Unjust or Unworthy Steward.

The story is of a certain rich man who had a steward who was called to account for wasting his master's goods. On being told that he was no longer a steward he says to himself: "What shall I do? I cannot dig; to beg I am ashamed." (v.3). He soon thinks of a solution to his problem: "I am resolved what to do, that when I am put out of the stewardship, they may receive me into their houses" (v.4).

He then proceeds to ingratiate himself with his master's debtors by letting them off with a part payment of their debts. His master acknowledges the astuteness of his business dealing and the success of its outcome (v.8) for by his action he gained friends on whom he could call for assistance when such was needed.

As a steward of all the benefits of the system of the Mosaic laws and religious ordinances the house of Judah had failed by allowing these to degenerate into empty formalities. The law, the prophets and the covenants were abused and rendered ineffectual by the time of our Lord's ministry and the steward was therefore unfaithful to his trust.

In that third verse the steward's statement is very appropriate as it describes exactly the character of the Jews down through the ages. They are not so much producers of goods but rather traders in them. They buy and sell and manipulate the financial markets and by their astuteness in their business practices they are never in the position of having to beg for their needs. They are very materially minded and over the years they have achieved positions of power in the banking houses of the world. They thus control the commercial life of nations and by their imposition of usury on all non-Jewish peoples they have caused financial troubles and distress among the nations. In their self-interest they are very wordly wise and have accumulated great wealth for themselves on earth. They are very much the children of this world (v.8) who build up treasures on earth which are, however, vulnerable and liable to sudden destruction. The children of light, to whom they are compared, are those who build up treasure in Heaven which is safe and indestructible.

In our Lord's teaching He declared that we could not worship God and mammon. Mammon is riches or material wealth and the pursuit of these things tends to occupy the minds and hearts of all who so indulge themselves, to the exclusion of spiritual matters. Self-interest excludes thoughts of others and their needs and is, therefore, the antithesis of the Commandment to: "Love your neighbour as yourself."

The stewardship of the kingdom requires obedience to the King, the upholding of His Commandments, Statutes and Judgements and the preaching of the gospels of Salvation and Redemption. Rather than self-interest it requires self-sacrifice in the service of others. The Jews have not fulfilled these requirements.

This parable is thus seen to portray in a material sense the great influence the Jews have in the affairs of all nations. Their astute, and at times unscrupulous, business practices have given them power in the world out of all proportion to their numbers. They have acquired for themselves through this power a disproportionately large share of the wealth of this world. As they have betrayed their trust in the stewardship of this material wealth, referred to as the 'mammon of unrighteousness', they are therefore declared to be unworthy to be trusted with what our Lord calls 'the true riches' (v.11). These riches are surely the fruits of the kingdom which can be had by all who worship the Lord.

Chapter 13

The Rich Man and Lazarus

Jesus follows this illustration with another which again relates to the house of Judah. Their identity is clearly indicated in the parable where it begins with reference in *Luke* ch.16 v.19 to a certain rich man 'clothed in purple and fine linen.' The purple identifies the royal line of Judah and the fine linen the priests of the tribe of Levi, portrayed in the symbolism of the parable as the secular and spiritual authorities in the kingdom.

The next character in the story is a certain beggar called Lazarus who was laid at the rich man's gate and who was 'full of sores' (v.20). Lazarus eventually died and 'was carried by the angels to Abraham's bosom' (v.22). The rich man also died and was buried. He is then said to be in hell and enduring torment and from this place he looks up and sees Lazarus in the company of Abraham. In his anguish the rich man asks Abraham to send Lazarus to comfort him. But Abraham reminds him that when he was enjoying the good things during his life Lazarus was poor and in need. Now the positions were reversed so that Lazarus was being comforted and the rich man was in torment. Besides this, he is told, there was a great gulf between them which could not be bridged. The rich man then asked if Lazarus could be sent to his house where he had five brothers, so that they could be warned of the torment they too might face. But he is told that 'they have Moses and the prophets' to whom they should listen and that if they failed to do so 'neither will they be persuaded, though one rose from the dead' (v.31).

Remembering that these parables in this study are all word pictures illustrating the different aspects and phases in the development of the kingdom one should not read into them what is not intended. This parable, therefore, does not infer that all rich people are wicked and descend into hell nor that all the poor of this world are good and go to heaven. It would be dishonourable to attribute such unfair partiality to God our Creator. So it is quite erroneous to regard this illustration as the basis for any doctrine on a future life beyond the grave, for this is not the subject of the parable.

The historical aspect of this story is accurately portrayed in the characterisation. The Jews of the House of Judah were symbolised in the rich man. They had the Scriptures, the Temple for their worship and the giving of their offerings and the heritage of the Hebrew religion handed down from the patriarchs of Israel. In contrast the House of Israel were reduced to poverty at that time. They were like displaced persons, some still living nearby in Asia Minor among heathen and idolatrous nations and subject to their ungodly ways, thus 'full of sores' as the parable relates. As they had ceased to exist as a separate nation the House of Israel had become lifeless as so aptly described in the parable of the dry bones in *Ezekiel*. Thus, in the story, the beggar dies and goes to Abraham's bosom.

As already stated the death of Jesus Christ brought redemption to the House of Israel. The old Covenant made at Mt. Sinai, which they broke, is now replaced with the new Covenant of Grace through faith and the covenant God made with Abraham (*Genesis* ch.13 vs.14-16) will be honoured through the redeemed House of Israel. This is the implication of the beggar Lazarus going to Abraham's bosom, comforted through the blood of Redemption shed for him on Calvary.

Names in the Bible all have significance and in this instance the name Lazarus means 'without help' (*Youngs Concordance*). This was very appropriate to Israel's situation prior to our Lord's death and resurrection. But after He had departed the apostles took the news of her Redemption to the dispersed people of Israel, some in Greece, in Italy then across Western Europe to those in the British Isles. Thus the beggar was comforted, the same expression, it will be noted, as that used by the prophet Isaiah (ch.40) referred to earlier in this study.

The rich man also dies and is buried. This brief statement in the parable is prophetic of the end of the kingdom of Judah in A.D.70. To lose this position of leadership among the twelve tribes and have the land taken over by a hostile power was torment indeed for the Jews. Their salvation would have been to believe what Moses and the prophets had proclaimed concerning the Messiah. But because they had failed to do so and then crowned this folly by rejecting Christ at His first advent there was this great gulf between them and the House of Israel, who welcomed the message of the apostles and accepted Christ as their Saviour and Redeemer.

Over the centuries the Jews have suffered a lot of persecution. Germany under Hitler in this present century is the most recent example of the torment of hell experienced by the 'rich man.'

In the parable the rich man tells Abraham that in his father's house he has five brothers. As he represents the House of Judah, which was comprised of the tribes of Judah and Benjamin with priests from the tribe of Levi, it might be wondered why he did not refer instead to ten brothers. It may be that the answer is simply that Judah was one of the six sons born to Leah, one of Jacob's wives, the other sons being Reuben, Simeon, Levi, Issachar and Zebulun. Thus it might be that he considered these five as true brothers compared to the half-brother relationship with the other six.

But this is attributing thoughts to a fictional character in the story when, instead, we should consider the thoughts in the mind of the story-teller, Jesus Christ. What message was He

82

conveying in this part of the parable? He was attributing to the rich man a request for a favour to be bestowed upon his brothers so that they might be spared the torment he was suffering.

"...send him (Lazarus) to my father's house...that he might testify unto them lest they also come into this place of torment" (vs.27-28).

He is told: "They have Moses and the prophets, let them hear them" (v.20).

What is the response? It is: "Nay father Abraham, but if one went unto them from the dead they will repent."

The response is the rejection of Moses and the prophets. When our Lord related this parable He was addressing the Pharisees and it was to their rejection of the words of Moses and the prophets concerning Himself that He was alluding in this story.

Christ's mission was to bring redemption to Israel through His death and thus replace the old Covenant made at Sinai with a new one, known as the Covenant of Grace. Grace is defined as 'free, undeserved favour' and it is only by God's grace and faithfulness that He has kept His promise to Abraham to preserve His people Israel. They were not worthy or deserving of this new Covenant through any action on their part. This is made very clear in the promised restoration of the kingdom made through the prophet Ezekiel (ch.36 v.22) "...I do not this for your sakes, O house of Israel, but for mine holy name's sake, which ye have profaned among the heathen wither ye went."

The significant point of the parable is the request of the rich man for favour to be shown to his brethren without the obligation of first accepting the Messiah Whose coming was foretold in the words of Moses and the prophets.

Some Bible students have studied the significance of numbers in the Scriptures and found that certain numbers are always associated with some particular aspect or principle in God's word. The number 'five' is thus found to be associated with God's Grace and His dealings with Israel. The reference to 'five brethren' should, therefore, be regarded as of little significance as a statement of family relationship, even though historically true. The real significance is in the use of the number 'five' in the illustration, our Lord thus revealing His awareness of the Jews' wish for God's Grace without the necessary acceptance of Him as their Saviour and Redeemer. It is doubtful that the Pharisees would recognise the significance of this numerical factor in the parable but it would be appreciated by the disciples, for the Lord revealed to them the mysteries of the kingdom.

In this parable we thus see the inclusion of one of the fundamental truths of the Christian gospel, which is that Grace comes only through faith in Christ Who is the Son of God. The words of Moses and the prophets are commended, by Divine authority, for our instruction and understanding regarding all matters relating to our Lord and His kingdom, just as much as they were to those living in His day. The writings of mortal man can become irrelevant and outdated but the Word of God remains relevant for all generations.

Chapter 14

The Good Samaritan

Many sermons on a moral theme have been preached from that well-known parable of the good Samaritan which is given in Luke's gospel, at chapter 10. It does indeed lend itself to such an interpretation but, again, its essential message relates to the kingdom. At the time this parable was given the Jews were known to be rather intolerant of those not of their faith and Christian charity, or its equivalent, was not a sentiment to be found in their character. Much of our Lord's teaching cut across the bigotry, the class and cultural barriers that existed in those times and it was partly for this reason that the Jewish hierarchy became so hostile to Him.

The man from Jerusalem who was attacked was presumably not a Jew for the priest and the Levite would surely not have withheld their aid from one of their own kind. But the Samaritan, one of those people who were rather despised by the Jews, was the one whose compassion was aroused at the sight of the man's distress. He bound the wounds of the injured man and took him to an inn where he left him in the care of the innkeeper. To him the Samaritan gave two pence as payment for the injured man's hospitality. The next day the Samaritan departed, promising that he would return at some later date and repay any further expense incurred by the innkeeper.

In the parable the man who is struck down and left lying injured in the road is symbolic of mankind who has suffered all kinds of trials and tribulations throughout history. The thieves referred to in the illustration represent the powers of evil who have caused all the suffering. The priest and the Levite are symbolic of the spiritual and political powers vested in the kingdom which the Jews had corrupted by the infusion of their own man-made traditions. Because of their negation of all the blessings which should have brought aid and comfort to a sin-filled world they were no longer worthy to be the custodians of kingdom authority. It was, therefore, taken from them as our Lord forewarned.

The great two-fold mission of Jesus Christ is covered in this seemingly simple parable, more surely revealed by having the key of the kingdom identity seen in the development of the British people (berith-ish = covenant man; *Youngs Concordance*).

In *Exodus* ch.30 v.13 the half shekel was the ransom price demanded by God for the souls of all the adult population in atonement for their sins. The two pence given by the good Samaritan was the equivalent coinage in the currency of the day to the half shekel. Thus the two pence represented the Lord's offering for the sins of mankind and for the redemption of Israel. Without paying the required price the injured man could not have been restored to health, nor could the innkeeper carry out the duty he had been given. The analogy thus clearly demonstrates that mankind could not be restored nor could Israel play her part in that restoration, except through the payment of the necessary price, our Lord's own sinless life given as an atonement for sin.

When the Samaritan departed he promised to return at a later date and repay "whatever more" the innkeeper had spent in caring for the injured guest. In the intervening years until now Israel has paid a further price, in the blood of martyrs and millions of other citizens in defence of the God-given principles which are contained in the Scriptures and which were the foundation of English Common Law. That further expense would be incurred by the innkeeper was acknowledged by the Samaritan in the promise of reimbursement which he gave.

The kingdom has been the target of Satanic attack throughout its life as the devil has endeavoured to thwart the plans of God. There is, therefore, much within the kingdom which is evil and offensive to Him. The faithfulness of the righteous and God-fearing throughout all generations has not been enough to defeat the powers of evil, the "principalities, powers, the rulers of darkness...spiritual wickedness..." referred to by St. Paul in his letter to the Ephesians. However, when Christ returns He has promised to reimburse the cost incurred by the kingdom in maintaining its witness. This will be fulfilled when, at His second advent, all who gave their lives for Him, in service or in sacrifice, will be repaid by resurrection to everlasting life in the new age.

The kingdom will be restored to righteousness and peace under the rule of Jesus Christ, the King of kings. The restoration and cleansing of the kingdom is graphically described in the prophecy of *Ezekiel* ch.11 vs.18-20, where we again see the 'I will' of God.

"...and I will take the stony heart out of their flesh, and will give them an heart of flesh: that they may walk in my statutes, and keep mine ordinances and do them; and they shall be my people, and I will be their God."

Chapter 15

The Two Debtors

In the gospel of *Matthew,* ch.18, the writer records Peter's request for guidance on the matter of forgiveness. Jesus answers his query with a statement which would at first seem strange if it was simply taken as read. The Lord told Peter that he should not just forgive a brother seven times for sinning against him but seventy times seven. It might be understood to mean that however often a person offended against one that person should be forgiven as long as he or she repented and asked forgiveness. Undoubtedly there is a moral principle involved here for all Christians to observe in their daily lives. The question Peter asked was based on a personal relationship and our Lord's answer clearly indicated the importance He placed on forgiveness in such relationships. He reiterated this position at the end of the parable which followed His statement.

However, to state that specific figure of 'seventy times seven' Jesus must surely have intended to convey something of particular significance particularly as He immediately goes on to relate another parable, linking it directly to that statement:

"Therefore is the kingdom of heaven likened unto a certain king which would take account of his servants" (v.23).

Seventy times seven is, of course, 490 and it will be found that this was the number of years from the completion of the new temple in Jerusalem, under Ezra's direction, in 458 B.C. to the crucifixion of Christ in A.D.33.* In *Daniel* ch.9 vs.24-27 the prophet records the words of the angel Gabriel which

---

* These dates are taken from the *Scofield Reference Bible.*

were told to him, prophesying what was termed a seventy week period of time in the life of the kingdom of Judah which would culminate in the death of our Lord and the anointing of the apostles by the Holy Spirit. Seven weeks is 490 days and in the Divine day-for-a-year scale ("I have appointed thee each day for a year." *Ezekiel* ch.4 v.6) it is the 490-year period of the prophetic vision.

The importance and, indeed, the need for forgiveness was known and accepted by leading figures in Israel's history. In II *Chronicles* ch.6, from vs.14-42, we read Solomon's wonderful prayer of dedication of the temple. It is a remarkable prayer and in a way prophetic, as though the king in his wisdom was aware of the character of his people and could foresee a time when, for their sins, they would become captives under a foreign power. Thus looking ahead to such a situation (vs.36-39) the king prays that God will even then hear the prayers of His people if they repent and turn back to Him.

Turning again to the prophet Daniel, who was with the house of Judah during their captivity in Babylon, we read (in ch.6 v.10) that the prophet prayed on behalf of the people that God would forgive them and restore them to their homeland. The kingdom was in part restored to the promised land and we read in the books of Ezra and Nehemiah that the people were led in prayers of confession and praise in remembrance of all that God in His faithfulness had done for them. Thus they began that 490-year period which brought to fulfilment the promise of the Messiah coming from their midst for His mission as Saviour and Redeemer.

The parable is again about a king who decides to review the work of his servants and on doing so he finds that one particular servant owes him a large amount, 'ten thousand talents.' The king demands that this servant should sell all his possessions so that he can repay the debt. But the servant pleads for mercy and for time, promising to repay all that he owes. The king responds with compassion and frees the servant from the debt.

The same man finds that he is owed a comparatively small sum by one of his fellow servants. Instead of showing similar compassion as was shown to him he has the unfortunate debtor thrown into prison until the debt is paid off. The other servants reported this to the king who was greatly angered by this action "...and delivered him to the tormentors till he should pay all that was due to him' (v.34).

In this illustration the king represents our Lord and the servants are the twelve tribes of Israel. The servant who owed so much to the king represents the house of Judah for, as has already been shown in this study, they were the most strongly condemned by God for their treachery and misuse of their position of stewardship of the kingdom. This situation reaches its climax in their rejection of our Lord's teaching and their instigation of His crucifixion. In this action they placed themselves ever deeper in debt yet, in His compassion, our Lord's words on the cross were the ultimate in practising what He Himself had preached:

"Father forgive them for they know not what they do."

As Peter had brought up the subject of forgiveness it appears that Jesus took the opportunity to use the occasion to announce in advance His plea to the Father on behalf of the people of Judah whom He identified in that appropriate numerical symbolism.

However, this did not mean that the Jews would escape the consequences of their unrighteousness and, as already stated, their position of authority and leadership in the kingdom would be taken from them and vested in the resettled nation of Israel in the western world. In the prophecy of *Jeremiah*, ch.30, we read in verse 11 of the situation in which God's judgement on all the tribes of Israel – signified by the collective name of 'Jacob' – is again seen to be tempered with mercy;

"...and I will not make a full end of thee; but I will correct thee in measure and will not leave thee altogether unpunished."

The principle of 'correction in measure' was undoubtedly applied to the Jews when their kingdom was destroyed and a great number of the people perished at the hands of the invading Romans. However, a 'full end' of them did not occur and many survived, some remaining in Palestine, but with a large proportion fleeing into other lands and subsequently earning for themselves the appellation 'the wandering Jews.' Many of these stateless people settled in Europe and other parts of the world. They achieved for themselves positions of power and influence in the countries wherein they settled. In more recent times their increasing hold over the commercial life of Britain, the U.S.A. and the British Commonwealth through their control of international finance is aptly portrayed in this parable.

The Jews, whose great debt had been forgiven by Christ on the Cross, have put their fellow servant Israel in debt to them, imprisoned within their financial constraints and being impoverished in their efforts to service the debt. Due to their imposition of usury all efforts by our governments to pay off these debts involve an increasing burden of taxation on all the people yet the debt is never fully repaid. When the Lord returns to rule in His kingdom the injustice of this action by the Jewish banking cartel will be condemned and they shall be 'delivered to the tormentors.'

Here again we see a repetition of Scripture terminology, for the rich man who wished to have the help of Lazarus was said to be in 'torment.' For these Jewish bankers their torment will be their loss of financial power and control over the nations and the recompense they have to make to those they had enslaved in their financial grip.

As with the elder brother in the parable of the prodigal son so also is the servant here seen to be refused a place in the kingdom until he has paid his debt to the King. Thus the Jews of the house of Judah are again depicted as remaining outwith the kingdom until they have repented and accepted the risen Lord as Saviour and Redeemer. This understanding of the Scriptures is no doubt contrary to the general teaching of orthodox Christian doctrine, which proclaims that Jews and Israelites are one and the same. It is hoped that in this study such has now been clearly shown not to be the case. Indeed it should perhaps be emphasised that the return of less than fifty thousand from Babylon to Judea under Ezra and Nehemiah were only a small proportion of the house of Judah, the majority remaining in Babylon until that empire was overthrown. Thereafter, like their brethren of the house of Israel, there was a general migration westwards to join them on the North Sea fringe and in the British Isles.

It is also evident that earlier, pre-captivity migrations from among the twelve tribes had taken place. This has already been shown in this study when Zedekiah's daughter, Tamar, was found to have married into another branch of the tribe of Judah who had, some time previously, settled in Ireland.

The great importance of that remnant of the house of Judah, who became known as 'Jews' (a corruption of the title Judahite), was the inclusion of descendants of the royal line of David within their number. It was only through them that God could fulfil His promise to redeem His fallen creation and His covenant-breaking kingdom. From amongst these Jews came the first evangelists who spread the gospel of the kingdom following their anointing by the Holy Spirit. They were Galileans, as Scripture informs us, and mainly of the tribe of Benjamin. It was among the people of that area in northern Judea where Jesus received the most sympathetic response during His ministry.

It is known that the Jews in the years before our Lord's first advent won many converts to their faith, including people of other races with whom they intermarried. Amongst these were Idumeans, a people who lived in the land south of the Dead Sea. They were former enemies of Israel and were a ruthless and warlike people. Descendants of Esau, and also known as Edomites (Idumean being the Greek form of that name), their racial characteristic influenced to a large extent that of the Jews through intermarriage between them. The Pharisees were a product of this racial mix and their hostility to our Lord was very much a result of this inherent characteristic. This Edomite infusion into the Jewish race had a visible effect in what has come to be known as the 'Jewish nose.' The swarthy complexion and prominent nose of the Edomites became a feature of the Jews who were the product of intermarriage. Such distinction of countenance as a mark of identification was foretold by the prophet Isaiah:

"For Jerusalem is ruined and Judah is fallen; because their tongue and their doings are against the Lord, to provoke the eyes of His glory. The shew of their countenance doth witness against them, and they declare their sin as Sodom, they hide it not. Woe unto their soul for they have rewarded evil unto themselves" (*Isaiah* ch.3 vs.8-9).

These Jews with their distinctive alien appearance and character were condemned in forceful terms in *The Revelation* of Jesus Christ. In that final book of the Word of God He referred to the 'blasphemy of them which say they are Jews, and are not, but are the synagogue of Satan' (*Revelation* ch.2 v.9).

Having this unrighteous element within the kingdom of Judah, one which had so much power and influence over the people, it can be seen that such a situation would not be permitted to continue. Therefore judgement came upon the kingdom when it was destroyed in A.D.70.

There were, of course, Jews who had, for the most part, kept to the laws of God and maintained their racial purity and it was from amongst those that Jesus Christ came at His first advent. There are today still those of the Jewish community who are fair-haired and blue eyed and without the distinctive features of the Edomite strain. Therefore when reference is made to 'the Jews' the distinction of the true Jew by race from the Jews that are such through religious or political persuasion should be clearly kept in mind.

Further enlightenment on the origins of modern Jewry is given by numerous authoritative researchers into racial sources. The Jews are found to be divided into two main sections, the Ashkenazim and the Sephardim. The majority of the Jews today, around 90 per cent, belong to the former and are predominantly brachycephalic (broad headed). They are mainly European Jews and migrants from thence to America and elsewhere. The Sephardim are dolichocephalic (long headed) and constitute only about 10 per cent of Jewry. They are much less racially mixed and generally akin to the Anglo-Saxon and Celtic racial type and character.

The Ashkenazim have the propensity to seek power and control over peoples and nations and it was the element of Jewry who were referred to in the parable of the husbandmen who, on seeing the son of the householder, said: "This is the heir; come let us kill him and let us seize on his inheritance." (*Matthew* ch.21 v.38). The kingdom, our Lord's inheritance in this Christian dispensation, has indeed been seized or controlled to a great extent by those who may call themselves Jews but who are such in name only. Their power and authority and their influence in the policy decisions of governments has directed the course of individual and national life for many generations. Any opposition to, or criticism of, modern Jewry and their methods, by those who see them to be the cause of so much of the injustice and hardship of the world, brings down upon such critics the accusation of anti-Semitism.

Strictly speaking the adjective Semitic is descriptive of all who are descended from Shem, one of Noah's three sons. The Ashkenazim are, as already stated, of mixed racial origins, some of whom were descended from Japheth, a brother of Shem. Thus they cannot in truth claim to be purely Semitic peoples. In contrast the Anglo Saxon and Celtic race, whose ancestry goes back to Abraham, are Hebrew in origin as Abraham was of that race. (*Genesis* ch.14 v.13). The name 'Hebrew' was derived from Eber, a descendant of Shem which means, then, that the Israelites and their descendants were, and are, themselves truly Semitic. It is hardly surprising, therefore, that those who, by our Lord's own definition are of the Synagogue of Satan, should encourage such a deception.

There has been, and still is, much confusion over the identity and origin of the people known as Jews and it has been felt necessary at this point in this study to go briefly into their history and highlight the two distinctive sections of these people with their different roles on the world stage. They have in common their rejection of Jesus Christ as the Messiah but orthodox rabbinical Jews still retain the Old Testament Scriptures as the foundation of their faith. However, even this Jewish faith, like its Christian counterpart, has been affected by modernistic creeds which many have adopted, whilst yet other Jews have become avowed atheists.

It is wrong, therefore, to think of 'the Jews' as being a homogeneous people, either from a racial, religious or even cultural standpoint. This is a fact they themselves acknowledge for they have always been zealous proselytisers amongst other communities and peoples, even back in pre-Christian ages. It was in those early years that the Ashkenazim strain of Jewry came into being. Marriage with people from outside the kingdom was contrary to the Divine Law in Israel. So by breaking this law and bringing into being the more unscrupulous strain of the Ashkenazim the words of the prophet Isaiah have been fulfilled in the persecutions of the Jews throughout the ages: "...for they have rewarded evil unto themselves" (*Isaiah* ch.3 v.9).

Chapter 16

The Ten Virgins

As has already been shown many of the parables bring us up to the end of the age, a time graphically described by Jesus Christ and recorded by the first three gospel writers in prophetic terms. His description of events in these last years of the 20th century, recorded in *Matthew* ch.24, describe a situation which is unique to this present generation. The critical situation is vividly portrayed in our Lord's declaration: "...except these days be shortened there should no flesh be saved." Literally the end of all life on this planet. The signs of such a potentially disastrous situation are now only too clear and modern prophets of doom have warned that life in this world will come to an end early in the 21st century. Humanly speaking their prognosis is undoubtedly justified. However, such prophets leave God out of their reckoning.

Having warned of this possible destruction if nothing was done to prevent it our Lord goes on to declare that action will be taken to avert disaster: "...but for the elect's sake those days shall be shortened." Of all the nations only Israel were ever referred to as 'elect' (*Isaiah* ch.45 v.4). Thus he foretells of the intervention of behalf of His people when they are faced with this crisis, even although it is the consequence of their own unrighteous actions.

A large proportion of God's word is prophetic but it is not given to us to be used like a crystal ball in a search for dates or times in the future. In the gospel of *John* (ch.14 v.29) Jesus speaks to His disciples concerning His coming death and resurrection, saying:

"And now I have told you before it comes to pass, that when it comes to pass ye might believe."

There is a principle here which applies to all prophecies, so that those applying to these last days prior to Christ's second advent should be watched for and be recognised as and when they have taken place. In answer to the disciples' question regarding the signs to be expected at the time of His coming again our Lord warned of: "...wars and rumours of wars...famines, pestilences and earthquakes in diverse places...iniquity (lawlessness) shall abound, the love of many shall wax cold."

The last sign in that catalogue is very appropriate, as wax which has become cold also becomes hard and thus describes the attitude of people towards each other in this materialistic and selfish age. All the signs listed are more in evidence now than ever before. In Mark's gospel, where the same signs are given by our Lord, He ends His discourse by saying: "What I say unto you I say unto all, Watch."

This call for awareness and watchfulness is the theme of the next parable in this study, for it is a parable dealing mainly with the Lord's second advent and the days leading up to it. It is the well known parable of the ten virgins given in *Matthew* ch.25.

There were ten bridesmaids who were awaiting the arrival of the bridegroom and having their lamps with them. Five were wise and took spare oil with them in case their lamps went out, but the other five were foolish and took no such precaution. The bridegroom's arrival was announced at midnight and the bridesmaids were roused from their sleep. The wise ones were able to replenish their lamps but the foolish five found their lamps had gone out and, with no spare oil to relight them, begged the others to share their oil with them. The wise ones refused and told the others to go and buy more oil. They did so but in consequence were late for the marriage and found themselves excluded from it. The reply to their request for admittance was" "Verily I say unto you I know you not."

In this further parable of the kingdom the reference to 'ten virgins' identifies the people as the ten-tribed kingdom or house of Israel. It follows the end-of-the-age conditions Jesus had described in the previous chapter of *Matthew* and in the parable the bridegroom is analogous of the Lord Himself. The bridesmaids represent the Christians within the kingdom who, through their knowledge and faith, would be expecting and waiting for the arrival of the bridegroom.

In the illustration it is related that the bridegroom 'tarried.' The disciples were expecting the imminent restoration of the kingdom in their own lifetime but, of course, it was not to be. There was a waiting period while the kingdom became established in 'the appointed place' and the gospel of the kingdom made known. Many Christians over the years have watched and waited for Christ's return, some even trying to pinpoint the year and day of this coming event, referring to the prophetic statements of Scripture to support their view. However, they have ignored or forgotten our Lord's own words concerning it when He said:

"But of that day and hour knoweth no man, no not the angels which are in heaven, neither the Son but the Father."

He also declared in *The Revelation:* "Behold I come as a thief. Blessed is he that watcheth."

A thief comes unexpectedly and will only be spotted by someone who is actually on watch looking out for such an intruder. As the ten bridesmaids fell asleep when, after some time had elapsed, there was still no sign of the coming of the bridegroom, so also have a great many Christians ceased to keep alert for the indications of the Lord's imminent return. With many of them their professed belief in the second coming is qualified by their assertion: "...but not in my lifetime."

Of the ten bridesmaids we are told that five took with them spare oil for their lamps. So although they, too, slept they were better prepared than the others. Remembering that this is a parable we should look for the meaning behind the symbolism which is used. What did the lamps actually represent? There is really no need for any speculation on this point for it will be found once again that the Bible is its own interpreter. In *Psalm* 119 the following explanation will be found: "Thy word is a lamp unto my feet and a light unto my path."

In the second epistle of *Peter* ch.1 v.19 it will be found that the apostle is even more specific when he wrote:

"We have also a more sure word of prophecy, whereunto ye do well that ye take heed as unto a light that shineth in a dark place..."

So the Bible, with its books of the law and the prophets for our instruction and guidance, is our lamp.

Then there is the oil which the wise prudently took with them to replenish their lamps. It has been suggested by some that it represented the work of the Holy Spirit. The guidance of the Holy Spirit is certainly a requirement for our better understanding of God's word. However, in the parable the oil is something which could be purchased with money.

"...go ye rather to them that sell and buy for yourselves." admonished the wise bridesmaids.

The Holy Spirit is not someone who can be bought. This was clearly shown in the Acts of the Apostles when Simon, seeing the work of the Holy Spirit in the laying on of hands, offered Peter more money for that power.

"But Peter said unto him: Thy money perish with thee, because thou hast thought that the gift of God may be purchased with money."

The Bible again leads us to an explanation of this particular symbolism, found in the book of *Proverbs* ch.23 v.23.

"Buy the truth and sell it not, also wisdom and instruction and understanding."

These words bring to mind again our Coronation service and the words of the archibishop, as he hands the Bible to the new monarch and says of it: "Here is wisdom, this is the royal law, these are the lively oracles of God." Wisdom, instruction and understanding. Perhaps that verse in *Proverbs* was the inspiration for those words spoken by the archbishop in the Coronation service. These are the essentials for life in the kingdom of God, they are contained in the Scriptures and these can be purchased with money. One can also buy books by researchers and scholars which support the accuracy and authenticity of the Bible and provide confirmation of its Divine inspiration. They assist us when we do as St. Paul advised Timothy:

"Study to show thyself approved unto God; a workman that needeth not to be ashamed; rightly dividing the word of truth." (II *Timothy* ch.2 v.15).

The bridesmaids are awakened in the middle of the night by the call heralding the arrival of the bridegroom. The middle of the night is the time of greatest darkness and is the most appropriate symbolism, in the spiritual sense, to depict the darkness of the kingdom just prior to Christ's return. It would undoubtedly be for this reason that this parable was given immediately following the end-of-the-age signs in the previous chapter of Matthew's gospel, a time of trouble and distress in the kingdom which is by then in a very low state.

The message of this parable is for watchfulness and preparedness in the kingdom. When the bridesmaids were awakened from their sleep by a shout of warning the five wise ones were able to trim their lamps so that they were not left in the dark. On the same principle Christians today, through studying the Scriptures alongside world events, will not be taken unawares when these events are seen to be those which were foretold as immediately preceding Christ's second coming. The five that were foolish and unprepared did not have sufficient knowledge or understanding of the relevance of the scripture signs. By the time they had acquired the necessary insight to the situation the great event, the marriage of the bridegroom and his bride, had begun. This marriage theme is like that of the king's son in *Matthew* ch.22 which has already been studied. In both these illustrations it will be found that only a limited number of guests actually attend the celebrations: "Many are called but few are chosen." The five foolish bridesmaids eventually knock on the door requesting permission to join the marriage feast but receive the reply from the bridegroom: "Verily I say unto you I know you not."

The prophetic Scriptures are very neglected by the average Christian and this is epitomised by the slumbering bridesmaids of the parable. The sudden awakening from their sleep to be confronted with the imminent arrival of the bridegroom shows that they remain in this state up until the last minute, as it were. Those who have been foolish and not kept abreast with world events and their fulfilment of Bible prophecy are thus caught unawares. Their efforts to remedy their situation are of no avail for the bridegroom refuses to recognise them when they finally realise what they had missed.

They were all awakened from their sleep by someone who calls out: "Behold the bridegroom cometh." Who makes this call? That person was obviously the one who was alert and watching and represents those who know the identity of the kingdom in the world today, who know the prophecies concerning the signs of the end of the age and recognise their relevance to national and international events. The Lord foresaw the period of slumbering in the kingdom and by His inspiration He has provided watchmen who will observe the signs and indications of His coming again and who have the responsibility of rousing the nation in due time.

Now is the time for the nation to be awakened from sleep to a knowledge of its identity and to the realisation of its destiny. The call of awakening must also be a call to repentance for the nation is steeped in unrighteousness and in dire need of cleansing. Evil knows no bounds and the few remaining Scripture-based principles which have been upheld until our present generation are now falling to modern ideologies. The whole fabric of society is affected:

"...avarice has grown with wealth and the frantic quest for pleasure is rapidly leading to the ruin of the whole fabric of society. In our ever accelerating downward course we have already reached a point where our vices and the cures for them are both intolerable."

That quotation from Pliny was a comment on the state of Roman society just before the Christian era began and it seems eminently appropriate to the state of the nation today.

Chapter 17

Stewardship of the Talents

There are, then, many signs of the end of this age and the watchmen have the responsibility of making the people in the kingdom aware of their significance. This burden of responsibility is portrayed in a further illustration immediately following the parable of the ten virgins.

The story is of a man travelling into a far country who gave his servants the care of his goods. To one he gave five talents, to another two talents and to a third he gave one talent then departed on his journey. It is related that the servant given five talents traded with them and made five more. Likewise the man given two talents gained two more but the man given the one talent merely set it aside and did nothing with it.

When the man returned at some later date he assessed their stewardship during the absence. The servant who had increased his five talents by a further five was commended for his faithfulness. So also was the servant who had doubled his two talents. But the servant who had done nothing with his one talent was condemned for his negligence and was to be consigned to 'outer darkness.'

In this parable the man travelling to a far country is symbolic of our Lord who would depart from this world for a period of time. He left His servants, who represent His followers in the kingdom throughout the period of His absence, with the custody of His goods. They were the stewards of the kingdom which contained the throne of the Lord, in accordance with God's promise to king David. It also contained the Word of God with the law, the prophets and the gospels for the guidance and spiritual nourishment of the people of the kingdom. These were the goods over which the servants were given charge. All who have been blessed with the knowledge of this truth are duty bound to share it with others that they also might come to accept the Lord as Saviour and Redeemer, to keep His laws and to be aware of His promises and covenants with regard to His kingdom.

Some people are blessed with a deeper understanding of the words of Scripture than others, but however much we are able to grasp of the infinite wisdom and truth it contains we should share it with anyone who seeks knowledge of the kingdom. Those who faithfully and to the best of their ability fulfil this obligation will be rewarded by the Lord when He comes to rule in His kingdom.

In St. Luke's gospel (ch.19 vs.12-27) a similar parable is recorded, the theme being the same but with additional details included. The main characters here are 'a certain nobleman' and his 'ten servants'. Again the figure ten identifies the house of Israel but the house of Judah are also referred to, being those in the parable who reject the nobleman. The relevant statement occurs in verse 14 and was not mentioned in the similar parable related to Matthew. The passage reads: "But his citizens (subjects) hated him and sent a message after him saying – We will not have this man to reign over us."

This was the attitude of the Jewish hierarchy in Christ's day and their antagonism towards Him culminated in their demand – "crucify Him." The parable then goes on in similar manner to that related in Matthew's gospel, those who have been worthy stewards being commended while the one who was negligent was judged unworthy of a position in the kingdom. This time of judgement occurs after the nobleman's, i.e. the Lord's return at the end of this age. Then in Luke's account this is followed again by Christ's further reference to those who had rejected Him:

"But those mine enemies, which would not that I should reign over them, bring hither and slay them before me" (ch.19 v.27).

There is obviously no change of heart in these people so they must pay the price of their continuing enmity towards the Lord, an enmity which is characteristic of those whom He identified as of 'the synagogue of Satan.'

Orthodox Christian teaching dwells very much on the love of God and His willingness to forgive those who sin and err in many different ways. It tends to be forgotten that forgiveness is very much dependent on the repentance and change of heart of the sinner. Certainly on a personal level Christians are instructed to 'turn the other cheek' in response to unkindly acts perpetrated against them. However this tolerance of evil has been taken beyond what can be justified at the community or national level. At that level the judgements of God, as contained in the Divine law, come into effect and it can only be to the detriment of the quality of life of the nation if these are not enacted. This is exemplified in the present state of iniquity and apostasy in the nation where so much that is condemned under God's law is now tolerated and, in some instances, actually encouraged.

To a society steeped in unrighteousness the judgements of God appear harsh and contrary to their concept of a God of love. They find unpalatable the references in Scripture to the God who ordered, or carried out at His own hand, the destruction of whole communities of people. To find that God can hate: "Jacob have I loved but Esau have I hated" (*Romans* ch.9 v.13, in which Paul quotes from *Malachi* ch.2 vs.2-3) is contrary to their vision of a 'Father Christmas' type of deity who smiles benevolently on all their activities regardless of their consequences.

God does not have to justify Himself to us. It is we who, by faith, must accept that there "is no God else beside Me; a just

God and a Saviour." (*Isaiah* ch.45 v.21), that He does nothing without good reason and that His prime concerns are the preservation of His creation and His kingdom.

Chapter 18

The Judgement of the Nations

Judgement is the province of God alone on all matters pertaining to the kingdom. Throughout Scripture it is much in evidence as He views the deeds of mankind who has abused the freedom of choice laid before him by his Creator. The two parables which have just been studied were part of our Lord's discourse given on the Mount of Olives. Following His account of the servants and the goods entrusted to their care He goes on to state what will take place after He has returned in glory accompanied by His angels. It is clearly a time of judgement for the nations of the world. Judgement of the kingdom will have taken place when the tares will have been separated from the wheat and destroyed. Now we are given an illustration of separation of nations and peoples classified as sheep and goats. The sheep are those nations which are gathered to be placed on the King's right hand and given a place under kingdom authority. They are told that they have earned this because they had given food, drink, shelter, clothing, help during illness and comfort when imprisoned to all who had need of these services. The goats are those nations who were placed on the King's left hand and condemned for not providing these services when and wherever they were required.

History confirms that the nations of the Anglo-Saxon and Celtic peoples have been in the forefront of missionary and charity work throughout the world. Over the years their response to situations in which people have been the victims of natural disaster or political persecution has been the main source of aid. On the spiritual side more than 90 per cent of the missionary work in foreign lands has come from Great Britain and her Israel brethren.

Thinking on this spiritual aspect the words of our Lord in His sermon on the mount (*Matthew* ch.5) come to mind. He said on that occasion:

"Blessed are they who hunger and thirst after righteousness, for they shall be filled."

The spiritual food and the water of eternal life are the more important aspects of the gospel, even although the practical and material things of this life also matter.

The spiritual nakedness of the individual, an unenviable condition, can be overcome by putting on 'the whole armour of God,' which not only covers but protects the individual from the attentions of false goods and creeds. (*Ephesians* ch.6 v.11). Those who are spiritually sick, due to lives spent in unrighteousness, or imprisoned by the constraints of false doctrines, can be, and have been, released from their unpleasant state by the light of the gospel of Jesus Christ being taken to them.

There are many nations and peoples who live under repressive regimes where religious or political dogmatism deliberately excludes the light and truth of God's word and persecutes those who seek to embrace it. Of such are the goat nations and they are known to the Lord for they cannot hide their deeds from Him. That their unregenerate state persists in spite of the preaching of the gospel of the kingdom world-wide is no serious reflection on the missionary zeal of those dedicated servants of the Lord who have endured danger and hardship to be His witnesses.

God has provided His word for our benefit and blessing and has inspired men and women to proclaim His truth to all who will listen. But He is well aware that Lucifer is increasingly active on the earth as his limited period of influence draws to its close (*Revelation* ch.12 v.12). We are almost at the end of this age and the beginning of the new age under Christ's reign. God has made all necessary provision to counter the work of the Devil and the consequences of man's folly. All nations have had time to learn about the God Who has created all things and Who gave His Son to be a ransom for the sins of mankind and the redemption of His people Israel. They have had time to make their choice, whether it be 'good and life or evil and death'. Now the time for the judgement of the nations is about to come. The kingdom will be cleansed and the world saved from its threatened destruction. Israel will be regenerated and, under Christ the King, will begin to fulfil her destiny of leading all people back to the Lord. For this was the reason for her creation as promised to our forefather Abraham, recorded in *Genesis* ch.22 vs.16-18:

"By myself have I sworn, saith the Lord, for because thou hast done this thing and hast not withheld thy son, thine only son; That in blessing I will bless thee, and in multiplying I will multiply thy seed as the stars of the heaven and as the sand which is upon the sea shore...*And in thy seed shall all the nations of the earth be blessed* because thou has obeyed my voice."

This future time of blessing is foretold in the prophecy of Micah, in the first few verses of chapter 4:

"And many nations shall come, and say, Come and let us go up to the mountain of the Lord, and to the house of the God of Jacob; and he will teach us of his ways and we will walk in his paths; for the law shall go forth of Zion, and the word of the Lord from Jerusalem. And he shall judge among many people and rebuke strong nations afar off; and they shall beat their swords into plowshares and their spears into pruning hooks; nation shall not lift up sword against nation, neither shall they learn war any more."

This is a glorious prospect as the world flounders aimlessly in the darkest hour of the night, a prospect which will shortly become a reality when the King of kings and Lord of lords returns in power and glory:

110

"...and the government shall be upon his shoulder; and his name shall be called Wonderful, Counsellor, The mighty God. The everlasting Father, The Prince of Peace. Of the increase of His government and peace there shall be no end, upon the throne of David and upon His kingdom, to order it, and to establish it with judgement and with justice from henceforth even for ever. The zeal of the Lord of hosts will perform this." (Isaiah ch.9 vs.6-7)

What more could mankind wish for? This is no dream or false hope but the promise of God.

Conclusion

In this study of the parables of the kingdom of God it has been shown that there is a continuity of purpose in the scheme of our Creator, the God of Israel, revealed in the pages of His word. The Bible contains the details of two similar or parallel situations. First there is the account of the creation of man as a perfect being. There is then recorded man's fall from grace through Satanic influence, but immediately there follows the promise of the provision of a Saviour Who would preserve him from the consequence of that fallen state. The apostle John confirmed that that promise was fulfilled in Jesus Christ, in those words which are at the heart of the Christian faith:

"For God so loved the world that He gave His only begotten Son, that whosoever believeth in Him should not perish but have everlasting life" (*John* ch.3 v.16).

This love of God is not emotional or sentimental as is so often the case with human love. His is a deep caring love which is really beyond our understanding. But, like our own, His love calls for a response in kind, so He desires mankind to respond to it freely and of their own choosing. He does not wish to have a world full of puppets, which would obey His every command but be unable to reflect His love. He wants intelligent human beings to put their trust in Him, having seen the clear evidence of the shortcomings of their own man-made laws and standards.

As an aid to mankind making the right choice God created a nation of people who were to demonstrate the benefits to be enjoyed by keeping the Divine code of law placed before them. The second situation, which is a parallel to that of the fall of man, was the fall from grace of that nation Israel, who broke the covenant made with God at Mt. Sinai and, as a consequence, were expelled from the promised land, just as

Adam was expelled from Eden. For the preservation of the kingdom from total extinction the same intercessor was promised Who would redeem them that they might fulfil their mission at some later date.

The husband and wife relationship between God and Israel, with the bill of divorcement (*Jeremiah* ch.3 v.8) illustrating the break in their partnership, was the situation portrayed in the first parable of this study, that which was related in the prophecy of Hosea. The death of the husband being necessary before the divorced wife could legally become rebetrothed brings into focus the dual nature of the significance of our Lord's death on Calvary, being both the Saviour of mankind and the Redeemer of Israel. Here is a further parallel situation for, just as in *Genesis* ch.3 v.15 where the promise of a Saviour is given Who would bring restoration to a fallen human race, so also in *Hosea* ch.1 v.10 the promise of restoration is given for Israel. Such a restoration could only come through a Redeemer if the law on remarriage, referred to by St. Paul in *Romans* ch.7, was to be kept.

The Bible narrative is, from the time of the captivities onwards, the record of the progress of the kingdom from its rebellious state, through a period of punishment, relocation and reformation, culminating in the time of cleansing before it becomes acceptable again as the people of God. There have been many stages along that road and the parables have illustrated these more clearly than any other method might have achieved.

Nearly four thousand years of the history of the kingdom could not have been outlined more succinctly or briefly than has been done in the parable of the potter's vessel in *Jeremiah* ch.18. The disintegration of the kingdom and the expulsion of the people from their land is followed by their later reinstatement. This could hardly have been more graphically described than is done in the parable of the dry bones. The divided kingdom would in time be reunited and this is clearly shown in the joining of the two sticks in Ezekiel's prophecy. Progressing on to New Testament times the parable of the sower in Matthew's gospel describes the situation in the kingdom during this Christian dispensation. The stony ground represents the attitude of many people to the gospel of Jesus Christ which they reject. This response has implications which are more far-reaching than is realised, perhaps, by many people. It is clear that of those who have so rejected the Christian faith and teaching many achieve high office in government and in other influential positions within the nation. The consequences of this unrighteous influence on the life of the nation are all too apparent at the present time. They were foreseen and illustrated in the three parables which followed, with a further three showing God's hand in the counter-measures He put into effect. How different life would have been in the nation had the instructions given to Moses been re-enacted. (*Exodus* ch.18 v.21)

The two kingdoms of Israel and Judah are then depicted in character studies, illustrated in a remarkable way by the stories of two sons and brothers, showing their differences in nature and temperament. This has been reflected in the histories of the British people and of the Jews and the illustrations cover these histories right up to the end of this age. The final two parables deal almost entirely with this end time which will bring to a close the period of Satan's influence in the affairs of mankind and herald the new kingdom age under Christ's direction.

It must surely be a source of wonder to realise that so much of the history of the kingdom of God could be embraced by such comparatively short word pictures. In the foregoing brief summary their theme of reconciliation and restoration of the kingdom will be found to be complementary to the rest of the Scripture record. The prophets give more specific details about the kingdom relative to the people, locations, events and situations. The occurrence of their predictions is usually fulfilled at some specific time during the life of the kingdom, some in the then near future, others many years or even centuries later. The gospels and epistles record our Lord's ministry, His teaching and the building of the Christian church which is the body of Christ. *The Revelation* is again prophetic in its scope, looking ahead in time at the progression of the church within the kingdom as well as that of the kingdom itself which is the bride of Christ. Jesus Christ is both King and High Priest so the material and spiritual life of the kingdom is under His influence in this present dispensation and will be under His personal jurisdiction in the age to come.

The parables are, therefore, unique, having a message of their own in a form and style of their own. Analogy and symbolism form the framework of their composition thus giving them the appearance of mysteries. However, the key to unlock these apparent mysteries is the knowledge of the identity of the kingdom in the British and their kindred people overseas. This is the only key which makes sense of the symbolism used and truly reveals the depth of meaning they contain.

Undoubtedly the parables lend themselves to a secondary meaning of a more spiritual and personal nature and such expositions have their place in Bible study. However, that aspect has been outwith the scope of this study which has centred on the kingdom or national aspect of the parables, as it is believed that this is their principal message.

It is the earnest desire and prayer of the author that those who have read this study will have experienced, as he did, a sense of awe and wonder at the infinite vision of the mind of Almighty God revealed in His word. The parables are an integral part of that word and contribute to the understanding of God's plan and purpose for His kingdom. They contribute evidence to the fact that although the Bible is comprised of books by many different writers and compiled into one great volume by human agency, its contents throughout all its pages emanate from just one source. Therefore the Divine inspiration of all Scripture cannot reasonably be doubted and the exclamation of all who study them with an unbiased mind must sure be – Praise the Lord.